HIGHER ENGLISH LANGUAGE SKILLS

Mary M Firth
Andrew G Ralston

SCOTTISH
EXAMINATION
MATERIALS

HODDER
GIBSON
AN HACHETTE UK COMPANY

CONTENTS

INTRODUCTION

You can't revise for English interpretations.

Have *you* ever said that?

Obviously, because the interpretation section of Higher English is based on an "unseen" passage, you can't learn up the content in advance or memorise quotations.

But many students don't realise that questions on the *content* of the passage are only one aspect of interpretation work. At least as much emphasis is placed by the examiners on the *style* of language used. *Interpretation questions are not only asking you about **what** the writer is saying; they are asking you about **how** he or she says it.*

You *can* revise for these questions by training yourself to recognise the language features which help to make up a good written style.

For some authors, a good style comes naturally . . .

Thriller writer Edgar Wallace used to sit at his desk and produce 10,000 words a day, keeping up his strength by drinking thirty cups of tea and eating doughnuts. He wrote the screenplay for the film *King Kong* in nine weeks and composed so quickly that it was said that he could turn out a novel in the back of a taxi in a traffic jam.

. . . others find it much more difficult.

The nineteenth century French novelist Gustave Flaubert did not have a natural flair for writing and he would spend hours on a single sentence. He rewrote his most famous book *Madame Bovary* five times, never looking back at his previous version.

Every professional writer — whether he or she writes quickly and instinctively, like Edgar Wallace, or slowly and painstakingly, like Gustave Flaubert — has mastered the skills of word choice, sentence structure, tone, imagery, punctuation and so on. If you have never studied these techniques, you will not be able to answer questions on them and will end up making vague guesses. This book will explain the techniques, but it will do something else as well: it will train you to understand what the wording of questions is getting at, and will show you methods for approaching different kinds of questions.

If you work through this book systematically, by the time the Higher examination comes round you will have realised that

*You **can** revise for English interpretations!*

The authors would like to thank the following colleagues at Hutchesons' Grammar School, Glasgow, for their contributions to this book.

Jane Bulloch	Peter Colvin
Alec Dunlop	Dilys Lovell
Neil McDermott	Susan MacDonald

Papers used in this book are natural, renewable and recyclable products. They are made from wood grown in sustainable forests. The logging and manufacturing processes conform to the environmental regulations of the country of origin.

Orders: please contact Bookpoint Ltd, 130 Milton Park, Abingdon, Oxon OX14 4SB. Telephone: (44) 01235 827720. Fax: (44) 01235 400454. Lines are open from 9.00 – 5.00, Monday to Saturday, with a 24 hour message answering service. Visit our website at www.hoddereducation.co.uk. Hodder Gibson can be contacted direct on: Tel: 0141 848 1609; Fax: 0141 889 6315; email: hoddergibson@hodder.co.uk

Cover photo from Getty Images
Printed and bound by CPI Group (UK) Ltd, Croydon, CR0 4YY

A catalogue record for this title is available from the British Library

ISBN-13: 978-0-716-93224-6

PART ONE

Reading Skills

I : UNDERSTANDING THE MEANING

USING YOUR OWN WORDS

Some interpretation questions, like the example below from a recent Higher English examination paper, are designed to test whether you understand the basic meaning of the passage.

> Paragraphs 5, 6 and 7 deal with the "issues" referred to in line 69. In your own words, describe clearly what the three main issues are.
>
> **6 marks**

You will be asked to gather pieces of information which you must answer as far as possible in your own words. Simple words from the original passage *may* be used if there is no obvious alternative, but where there *is* an obvious alternative you should use one. Figures of speech in the original must always be put into plain language, and any non-standard expression, for example slang or archaisms (old-fashioned words), must be rendered in simple, formal, modern English.

✳   **Warning!** It is essential that you do not "lift" whole phrases or sentences from the original: these will not be awarded any marks, even though you have understood the question and the answer is correct.

WHAT THE EXAMINER IS LOOKING FOR

How much should you write? Every exam paper has what is called a "marking scheme": the number of marks which are allocated to each question. A marker cannot give you any more than the number allotted, and he will look for the required amount of information before awarding full marks to a question. Before you write your answer, you must take note of the number of marks available. For two marks, it is likely you will need to supply two pieces of information, but alternatively you might be required to give one detailed piece or four brief pieces.

It will be necessary for you to consider the wording of the question carefully for guidance. Occasionally, direct guidance may not be given and in this case you must use your common sense. Obviously, one brief piece of information will be inadequate for a four mark question; conversely, providing a ten line answer for a one mark question is unwise as you will waste valuable time.

Look at the following example.

> Thinking of Grandpa now, I recall the clouds of pungent smoke that he puffed from his favourite briar, his small shrewd eyes, still very blue, and the gleaming dome rising from fleecy tufts of white hair.
>
> *Question:* What three characteristics of "Grandpa" does the author remember? **3 marks**

Answer: She remembers her grandfather smoked a strong-smelling pipe. He also had intelligent bright blue eyes and a bald head with a little fluffy white hair.

Method: Understanding of "briar" is shown by using the more general term "pipe". The metaphor "gleaming dome" is simplified to "bald head". Since the word "eyes" is a common word with no obvious alternatives it may be used again. There are several possible alternative words for "shrewd", and "intelligent" is an acceptable one. Since "grandpa" is colloquial, the more formal "grandfather" is used in the answer.

If the question were worth only 1 or $1\frac{1}{2}$ marks, it could be answered more briefly: Her grandfather smoked a pipe, he had blue eyes, and was very bald.

FOR PRACTICE

Use the same method in the following examples, providing more or less detail as the number of marks suggests.

1. Jim scarcely recognised his long hair and grey cheeks, the strange face in a strange mirror. He would stare at the ragged figure who appeared before him in all the mirrors of the Columbia Road, an urchin half his previous size and twice his previous age.   Extract from *Empire of the Sun* by J.G. Ballard

Question
   Give **four** changes in his appearance that Jim notices when he looks at himself in the mirror.
2 marks

2. Myself, my family, my generation, were born in a world of silence; a world of hard work and necessary patience, of backs bent to the ground, hands massaging the crops, of waiting on weather and growth; of villages like ships in the empty landscapes and the long walking distances between them; of white narrow roads, rutted by hooves and cartwheels, innocent of oil or petrol, down which people passed rarely, and almost never for pleasure, and the horse was the fastest thing moving.

Extract from *Cider With Rosie* by Laurie Lee

Question
   (i) What was the nature of agricultural work during the author's childhood? **2 marks**
   (ii) What further clues are there to village life at that time? **3 marks**

3. When one came straight from England the aspect of Barcelona was something startling and overwhelming. It was the first time that I had ever been in a town where the working class was in the saddle. Practically every building of any size had been seized by the workers and was draped with red flags or with the red and black flag of the Anarchists; every wall was scrawled with the hammer and sickle and with the initials of the revolutionary parties; almost every church had been gutted and its images burnt.

Extract from *Homage to Catalonia* by George Orwell
© Mark Hamilton as the Literary Executor of the
Estate of the Late Sonia Brownell Orwell

Question
   Explain why the author found Barcelona astonishing. **4 marks**

4. Perhaps the greatest of all these masters of the latter part of the sixteenth century was Jacopo Robusti, nicknamed Tintoretto. He too had tired of the simple beauty in forms and colours which Titian had shown to the Venetians — but his discontent must have been more than a mere desire to accomplish the unusual. He seems to have felt that, however incomparable Titian was as a painter of beauty, his pictures tended to be more pleasing than moving; that they were not sufficiently exciting to make the great stories of the Bible and the sacred legends live for us. Whether he was right or not, he must, at any rate, have been resolved to tell these stories in a different way, to make the spectator feel the thrill and tense drama of the events he painted.

Extract from *The Story of Art* © 1995 E.H. Gombrich

Question
   (i) Why, according to the author, was Tintoretto dissatisfied with Titian's work? **3 marks**
   (ii) What was Tintoretto's own aim in portraying Bible stories? **1 mark**

5. The winter of 1542 was marked by tempestuous weather throughout the British Isles: in the north, on the borders of Scotland and England, there were heavy snow-falls in December and frost so savage that by January the ships were frozen into the harbour at Newcastle.

These stark conditions found a bleak parallel in the political climate which then prevailed between the two countries. Scotland as a nation groaned under the humiliation of a recent defeat at English hands at the battle of Solway Moss. As a result of the battle, the Scottish nobility which had barely recovered from the defeat of Flodden a generation before were stricken yet again by the deaths of many of their leaders in their prime; of those who survived, many prominent members were prisoners in English hands, while the rest met the experience of defeat by quarrelling among themselves, showing their strongest loyalty to the principle of self-aggrandisement, rather than to the troubled monarchy. The Scottish national Church, although still officially Catholic for the next seventeen years, was already torn between those who wished to reform its manifold abuses from within, and those who wished to follow England's example, by breaking away root and branch from the tree of Rome. The king of this divided country, James V, lay dying with his face to the wall.

Extract from *Mary, Queen of Scots* by Antonia Fraser

Question

    (i) What was noteworthy about the winter of 1542?   **2 marks**

    (ii) Identify **five** political problems that were facing Scotland.   **10 marks**

CONTEXT QUESTIONS

As well as showing that you understand the writer's general meaning, you will also be asked more precise questions, to show you understand particular words and phrases.

> Show how the first sentence provides a context which enables you to understand the meaning of the word . . .
>
> **2 marks**

In a so-called "Context" question, such as the one above, you will be asked *(a)* to explain the meaning of a word or phrase, and also *(b)* to show how you deduced the meaning from its placing in the text. This involves identifying clues in the sentences immediately surrounding the word. You must **quote** these words or phrases that provide the clues and briefly explain how they help to confirm the meaning.

If the context question is worth 2 marks, you will generally be awarded 1 mark for getting the meaning right and 1 mark for the quoted piece of evidence with a brief explanation. It is usually possible and advisable to quote two pieces of evidence and it is essential if the question is worth a total of 3 marks.

Here is a worked example:

> The rumour that Douglas was a prisoner was still *unsubstantiated*. There had been no witnesses to his bailing out of the plane, and no solid information could be expected from beyond enemy lines for weeks, perhaps even months.

Question

Show how the context helped you arrive at the meaning of the word *unsubstantiated*.   **2 marks**

Answer

The word "unsubstantiated" clearly means unconfirmed. (**1 mark**) The context makes this clear as it says there were "no witnesses" who could say for sure the news was true ($\frac{1}{2}$ **mark**), and the phrase "no solid information" also repeats the idea of there being no firm proof. ($\frac{1}{2}$ **mark**)

FOR PRACTICE

Give the meaning of the expressions printed in italics in the following examples and show how the context helped you to arrive at the meaning.

1. Silverstein was *implacable* in pursuing his revenge. After years of patient searching he had finally come face to face with his father's tormentor, and he showed no mercy.   **2 marks**

2. For two days the general *vacillated*. Should he give the order to advance, or should he allow his men to cling to their sturdy line of defence? This hesitation was to prove fateful.   **2 marks**

3. The position of the Stewart monarchs in the fifteenth and sixteenth centuries was peculiarly perilous in dynastic terms, for a number of reasons. In the first place chance had resulted in a total of seven royal *minorities* — there had been no adult succession since the fourteenth century — which had an inevitable effect of weakening the power of the crown and increasing that of the nobility.   **2 marks**

Extract from *Mary, Queen of Scots* by Antonia Fraser

4. Piero della Francesca, too, had mastered the art of *perspective* completely, and the way in which he shows the figure of the angel in foreshortening is so bold as to be almost confusing, especially in a small reproduction. But to these geometrical devices of suggesting the space of the stage, he has added a new one of equal importance : the treatment of light. In his pictures, light not only helps to model the forms of the figures, but is equal in importance to perspective in creating the illusion of depth.   **3 marks**

Extract from The Story of Art © 1995 E.H. Gombrich

5. Oliver's first play at the Edinburgh Festival was only a *qualified* success. True, the critics, including some who were frequently disdainful of new writers, were lavish in their praise, and the houses were pleasingly full in the first week. But by the second week the numbers attending had inexplicably fallen away and the show was lucky to break even.   **3 marks**

LINK QUESTIONS

Another type of question which is designed to test your understanding of meaning, as well as your appreciation of the structure of a text, is the so-called "link" question. You will be asked to show how one sentence provides a "link" in the argument. The "argument" need not be a discussion: here "argument" means the progression of ideas in a piece of writing and the link will join one idea to the next.

> "And therein lies the rub." Explain how this sentence acts as a link between the first paragraph and the two following paragraphs.
>
> **2 marks**

Usually, but not invariably, the "link" sentence will stand at the beginning of a paragraph. Part of the sentence — often, but not always, the first part — will refer back to the previous topic and another part of the sentence will introduce the new topic which follows. Such questions are usually worth 2 marks, which are awarded for correctly identifying the parts of the sentence that link back and forward and the two topics which they connect.

You should show the link by first **quoting** the part of the link sentence which refers back to the earlier topic, saying what this topic is, and then **quoting** the part of the link sentence which looks forward to the next topic, explaining what this is. The sentence may also begin with a linking word or phrase such as "but" or "however" which points to a change of direction and you should also comment on this. Look at the following example:

William Shakespeare is easily the best-known of our English writers. Virtually every man in the street can name some of his plays and his characters, and many people can also recite lines of his poetry by heart. However, despite our familiarity with his work, we know relatively little of the man himself. We do not know when or why he became an actor, we know nothing of his life in London, and almost nothing of his personal concerns.

Question

Show how the third sentence acts as a link in the argument.　　　　**2 marks**

Answer

The phrase "our familiarity with his work" looks back at the topic of how widely known Shakespeare's work is. The conjunction "however" which begins the sentence suggests a contrasting idea to follow. The second part of the sentence, "we know relatively little of the man himself", introduces the new topic, namely the things that are not known about Shakespeare, and a list of these follows this "link" sentence.

FOR PRACTICE

1. My mother was born near Gloucester, in the early 1880s. Through her father, John Light, she had some mysterious connection with the Castle, half-forgotten, but implying a blood-link somewhere. Indeed it was said that an ancestor led the murder of Edward II.

   But whatever the illicit grandeurs of her forebears, Mother was born to quite ordinary poverty. When she was about thirteen years old her mother was taken ill, so she had to leave school for good. She had her five young brothers and her father to look after, and there was no one else to help.

   Extract from *Cider With Rosie* by Laurie Lee

   Question

   Show how the first sentence in the second paragraph acts as a link in the argument.　　　　**2 marks**

2. Usually his mother would caution Yang the chauffeur to avoid the old beggar who lay at the end of the drive. This beggar had arrived two months earlier, a bundle of living rags whose only possessions were a frayed paper mat and an empty tobacco tin which he shook at passers-by. He never moved from the mat, but ferociously defended his plot outside the gates. Even Boy and Number One Coolie, the houseboy and the chief scullion, had been unable to shift him.

    However, the position had brought the old man little benefit. There were hard times in Shanghai that winter, and after a week-long cold spell he was too tired to raise his tin. After a heavy snowfall one night in early December the snow formed a thick quilt from which the old man's face emerged like a sleeping child's above an eiderdown. Jim told himself that he never moved because he was warm under the snow.

    Extract from *Empire of the Sun* by J.G. Ballard

    Question

    Show how the first sentence of the second paragraph acts as a link in the argument.

    2 marks

3. Mary Stuart was certainly rated a beauty by the standards of her own time: even John Knox described her as "pleasing". In her height, her small neat head, and her grace she resembled the contemporary ideal. It was the type of beauty which her contemporaries were already learning to admire in art, and could now appreciate in life, all the more satisfyingly because it was in the person of a princess.

    Not only the appearance, but also the character of Mary Stuart made her admirably suited to be a princess of France in the age in which she lived. Mary was exactly the sort of beautiful woman, not precisely brilliant, but well-educated and charming, who inspired and stimulated poets by her presence to feats of homage.

    Extract from *Mary, Queen of Scots* by Antonia Fraser

    Question

    Show how the first sentence of the second paragraph acts as a link in the argument.

    2 marks

4. The popular press found copy in Einstein. Newspaper photographers discovered a highly photogenic subject: his was a face of character: drooping, kindly eyes and wrinkles of humour surrounded by a leonine mane of hair. The habits of the man were a little irregular; already some of the characteristics expected of the absent-minded professor were beginning to show: he lived a simple life uncluttered by possessions and any of the outward trappings of success; when there was no need to be careful he was careless about his dress: sometimes he wore no socks.

All these qualities, combined with the publicised qualities of the man, kindliness, gentleness and warmth, would still not have been sufficient to turn Einstein into the international figure he was to become. The missing ingredient in this recipe for public fame was the apparently incomprehensible nature of Einstein's work. For a few years after the publication of the general theory of relativity only a limited number of scientists familiarised themselves with it in detail. Its abstruse nature became legend and absurd stories sprang up around its esoteric significance. It was even rumoured that there were few men in the world who were capable of understanding the theory.

Question

Demonstrate that the underlined sentence performs a linking function between the two paragraphs. **2 marks**

5. To us the sheer profusion of servants on the nineteenth century scene is striking. In 1851 between seven and eight per cent of the entire population of the country were servants, if we ignore children under ten. For women and girls the figure was over thirteen per cent and for them "service" was so much the commonest job that it accounted for nearly twice the number employed in the whole textile industry — by far the most important group of manufactures and one in which the majority of workers were female. It can almost be said that every family able to feed and clothe some sort of servant kept one. Within this vast and heterogeneous army conditions varied from the miserable child-of-all-work, sleeping on a sack under the stairs, in bondage for a few coppers a week and her wretched keep, to the great magnate's house steward, a prosperous member of the middle class.

Question

Show how the phrase underlined relates to what has gone before it and introduces a new idea to be developed in the remainder of the paragraph. **2 marks**

6. At school, Alastair had shown exceptional promise. He had excelled as a scholar, as a musician and on the games field; his popularity and talent had made him an obvious choice for head boy in his last year.

His university career made a sad contrast to the years as a golden boy. A baffling lack of commitment saw him fail his first year exams, and after a nervous breakdown early in his second year, he dropped out altogether.

Question

Show how the underlined sentence acts as a link. **2 marks**

II : APPRECIATING THE STYLE

In Section I we looked at some typical interpretation questions on the meaning or content of a passage. This section will concentrate on questions about *how* the passage is written, covering anything from sentence structure and punctuation to word choice and tone.

> ### TACKLING STRUCTURE QUESTIONS

Comment on the sentence structure of . . .

If you have already seen this question in a practice interpretation paper, you probably found it very difficult to answer. Most people will try to explain what the sentence means but the question is really about *how the sentence is put together.*

> Few write as an architect builds, drawing up a plan beforehand and thinking it out down to the smallest details. Most write as they play dominoes: their sentences are linked together as dominoes are, one by one, in part deliberately, in part by chance.
>
> *Arthur Schopenhauer, 19th century German philosopher*

It is probably safe to assume that the passages chosen for interpretations will have been carefully crafted by authors who take the "architect" rather than the "domino player" approach! To answer sentence structure questions properly you will need to be able to recognise

* different types of sentences

* how sentences can be separated or linked by different kinds of punctuation

* how the component parts of a sentence can be arranged according to various patterns

* how writers use different sentence structures

DIFFERENT TYPES OF SENTENCE

A sentence is a group of words which contains a verb and makes complete sense. A sentence can be:

✳ *a statement:*

John is sitting down.

Statements are usually used in narrative or factual writing.

✳ *a question:*

Is John sitting down?

Questions may be used in reflective or emotive writing.
Note especially the **rhetorical question**. This is a question to which no answer is really expected; it may have the effect of a strong statement:

What time of night do you call this?

✳ *an exclamation:*

John is sitting down!

Exclamations are used to convey a tone of amazement, shock or strong emotion.

✳ *a command:*

Sit down, John.

Commands are used in instructions and in writing aiming to persuade, such as advertisements.

✳ *a minor sentence*:

where the verb is omitted for dramatic effect — usually, but not always, this is some form of the verb 'to be'. For example

He looked in his rear-view mirror. Nothing coming.

The words "Nothing coming" do make complete sense, despite the missing verb; they are more than just a phrase. This is a more concise way of saying "Nothing was coming". Minor sentences are used for various reasons:

✳   to create impact, suspense or urgency
✳   to suggest informality
✳   as abbreviations in notes and diaries

PARAGRAPHING

Paragraphing is used to break writing into more easily digestible pieces. You may notice that pre-twentieth century writers often expect their readers to cope with longer paragraphs than writers of today! When a writer wishes his writing to have instant impact, or to be particularly easy to understand, he uses very short paragraphs. Examples of this might be advertisements or children's writing or articles for tabloid newspapers.

A new paragraph is used to mark a new stage in a narrative or argument. However, occasionally, paragraphing is used for effect. A single sentence paragraph may throw emphasis onto a statement or idea. It may be used to slow the action and create suspense. When you see an unusually short paragraph, you must consider what particular effect the author was aiming at.

FOR PRACTICE

Comment on the types of sentences used in the following pieces of writing. If the paragraphing is noteworthy in any way, say briefly what is special about it. Then discuss what effects the writers are aiming at.

1. Few vehicles are built more solidly or handle more surely than the Porsche 924S.

    Release the rear hatch, fold the rear seats and the 924S's sporting ability is superbly matched by its transporting ability.

    Fuel economy? Outstanding. Re-sale values? Reassuringly high. Warranties? Excellent. As you would expect.

    There is a two year unlimited mileage mechanical warranty. A ten year Porsche long-life anti-corrosion warranty. Not forgetting 12,000 mile service intervals.

    As you can see, the fun doesn't have to stop when the family starts.

2. I woke up with a head like a rodeo. Isn't it painful having fun? Mind you, last night hadn't been about enjoyment, just whisky as anaesthetic. Now it was wearing off, the pain was worse. It always is.

    I didn't want this day. Who sent for it? Try the next house. I burrowed into the pillow. It was no use. A sleepless pillow. What was it they called that? Transferred epithet? My teachers. They taught me everything I don't need to know.

    Extract from *Strange Loyalties* by William McIlvanney

3. Swallows?

    Dark air-life looping
    Yet missing the pure loop . . .
    A twitch, a twitter, an elastic shudder in flight
    And serrated wings against the sky,
    Like a glove, a black glove thrown up at the light,
    And falling back.

    Never swallows!
    Bats!
    The swallows are gone.   Extract from *Bat* by D.H. Lawrence

4. If you're interested in the RAF, do pay a visit to 602 Squadron museum. You'll be
    fascinated by this evocative tribute to a famous squadron. A visit takes the form of a
    tour led by a true enthusiast — so be prepared for an hour or so discussing the
    many pieces of memorabilia and old photographs on display; each picture tells a
    story and every item belonged to someone of note. Look out for the Battle of Britain
    tie and the book containing the names of men who took part in this famous battle —
    it is kept open on the page which shows the signatures of the survivors.

    Open: Wednesday and Friday, 19.30–21.30 (closed July and August).
                                        Extract from *Glasgow for Free* by Shipley and Peplow

5. He turned first to the stock-market prices and saw that Consolidated Cables had
    gone up a point. He turned next to the racing page. Scarlet Flower had come in
    fourth, which meant that was fifty quid down the drain. He read a review of a new
    play and then the sale-room news. He saw that a Millais had gone at Christie's for
    nearly eight hundred thousand pounds.

    Eight hundred thousand!

    The very words made him feel almost physically sick with frustration and envy.
                                        Extract from *The Shell Seekers* by Rosamunde Pilcher

6. Wednesday 15 February
    Unexpected surprise. Was just leaving the flat for work when noticed there was a
    pink envelope on the table — obviously a late Valentine — which said, "To the
    Dusky Beauty." For a moment I was excited, imagining it was for me and suddenly
    seeing myself as a dark, mysterious object of desire to men out in the street. Then I
    remembered Vanessa and her slinky dark bob. Humph.

    9 p.m. Just got back and card is still here.

    10 p.m. Still there.

    11 p.m. Unbelievable. The card is still there. Maybe Vanessa hasn't got back yet.
                                        Extract from *Bridget Jones's Diary* by Helen Fielding

7.   It grew louder — louder — *louder!* And still the men chatted pleasantly, and smiled. Was it possible they heard not? Almighty God! — no, no! They heard! — they suspected! — they *knew!* — they were making a mockery of my horror! — this I thought, and this I think. But anything was better than this agony! Anything was more tolerable than this derision! I could bear those hypocritical smiles no longer! I felt that I must scream or die! — and now — again! — hark! louder! louder! louder! *louder!* —

"Villains!" I shrieked, "Dissemble no more! I admit the deed! — Tear up the planks! — here, here! — it is the beating of his hideous heart!"

Extract from *The Tell-Tale Heart* by Edgar Allan Poe

PUNCTUATION

The punctuation used in the extracts above will have helped you to identify which sentences were statements, questions, exclamations, commands or minor sentences. While you are not likely to be asked in a Higher interpretation to explain why a sentence ends with a full stop or a question mark, you *will* be asked to comment on more subtle uses of punctuation — particularly inverted commas, colons, semi-colons and dashes.

Such questions might be asked directly, as in a recent Higher paper —

Show how the punctuation . . . is particularly helpful in following the argument at this stage.

— but your understanding of punctuation is more likely to be tested in the context of a general question on sentence structure.

Inverted commas are used for four main purposes:

1.   *To indicate the title of a play, book, television programme, etc.*
     "Macbeth"   "Sunset Song"   "The X Files".

2.   *For spoken words*
     "Did you have a good weekend?" asked Anne.

3.   *For quotations*
     As George Orwell said, "All animals are equal, but some are more equal than others".

4. *To mark off an individual word or phrase from the rest of the sentence.*

This might be done, for instance, if a word from a foreign language is used. It can also indicate that the author wants us to recognise that he is distancing himself from the use of a certain term which might be commonly used but which he does not necessarily agree with:

> In Victorian times foreign travel was the preserve of the "superior" classes of society.

The effect of the inverted commas here is rather like using the words "so called".

Colons, semi-colons and dashes

> A **colon** usually introduces a quotation, a list or an explanation or expansion of the previous statement.

> A **semi-colon** is generally a "finishing" pause, marking the end of a sentence but less firmly than a full stop does. It often comes between two statements which are closely connected, or which balance or contrast one another. It may also be used to separate a list of phrases.

> A **single dash** can be used to add on an extra piece of information very much as a colon does. It can also be used to indicate a breaking off in a sentence. A series of dashes might be used informally to convey an outpouring of ideas or emotions.

> **Two dashes** can mark off an extra, non-essential piece of information in the middle of a sentence — a technique known as **parenthesis**.

Example 1

At this time pass all the characters of the Spanish streets: the dark veiled women hurrying home from the priest; the Civil Guard whom nobody greets; gold-skinned sailors and strutting carters; goat-faced ruffians down from the hills; and old men with the hollow eyes of hermits — their skin stretched thin on chill, ascetic bones.

Extract from *As I Walked Out One Midsummer Morning* by Laurie Lee

Here the colon in the first line indicates that a catalogue of the "characters of the Spanish streets" is to follow. Each phrase describing a character or group of characters is separated from the others by a semi-colon. If the list of characters had been made up of single words rather than phrases, the writer might simply have used commas:

women, Civil Guards, sailors, carters, ruffians and old men.

The dash in front of the words "their skin stretched thin on chill, ascetic bones" shows that the author decided to add on an extra piece of description to reinforce the effect of "hollow eyes". ("Ascetic" means austere, spartan, self-denying).

Example 2

There were a king with a large jaw and a queen with a plain face, on the throne of England; there were a king with a large jaw and a queen with a fair face, on the throne of France.

In this example, a semi-colon is used in conjunction with repetition to create a balanced sentence (a technique known as **antithesis** which will be explained on page 25). The semi-colon comes exactly in the middle and emphasises the similarity between the occupants of the English and French thrones. However, the balance and repetition also serve to draw the reader's attention to the one difference between the respective monarchies — the queen of France was "fair" rather than "plain".

FOR PRACTICE

Discuss the purpose of the inverted commas, colons, semi-colons and dashes in the following extracts:

1.   Further on were stalls of slightly better-class goods: plaster dogs, single boots, oil-lamps, singing birds, flowers and gramophones with horns.

2.   By some casual mistake of book-keeping the sentence was never carried out; he was abandoned in jail and forgotten.

3.   Inside the Cathedral a splendid parade of priests, bishops, choirs, soldiers and city fathers moved to the high altar. The place was full; the singing poor.

Extracts from As I Walked Out One Midsummer Morning by Laurie Lee

4.   The small translucent bodies of the tiny, crab-like spiders were coloured to match the flowers they inhabited: pink, ivory, wine-red or buttery-yellow. On the rose-stems, ladybirds moved like newly painted toys; ladybirds pale red with large black spots; ladybirds apple-red with brown spots; ladybirds orange with grey-and-black freckles.

Extract from My Family and Other Animals by Gerald Durrell

5. As soon as we saw it, we wanted to live there — it was as though the villa had been standing there waiting for our arrival.

6. I got to my feet and shouldered my bags and nets; the dogs got to their feet, shook themselves, and yawned.

7. If I found something that interested me — an ant's nest, a caterpillar on a leaf, a spider wrapping up a fly in swaddling clothes of silk — Roger sat down and waited until I had finished examining it.

Extracts from My Family and Other Animals by Gerald Durrell

8. Steep rocky red mountains overhung the stream; great oaks and chestnuts grew upon the slopes or in stony terraces; here and there was a red field of millet or a few apple trees studded with red apples; and the road passed hard by two black hamlets, one with an old castle atop to please the heart of the tourist.

Extract from Travels with a Donkey by R.L. Stevenson

9. It always seemed dark, grey and cold, as if winter had already started, but we did not mind — it was so exciting — so many marvels to see, even the shows outside were wonders — people dancing and "tumbling" — the pictures of the fat woman, in evening dress, too, and we loved to watch the gold figures on the show-fronts beating their drums and triangles, supposedly in time to the band; they never were.

Extract from Oil Paint and Grease Paint by Dame Laura Knight

10. The old women peered up at me with red-rimmed, clouded eyes, and each tale they told was different: my ex-boss, the hotel-keeper, had been shot as a red spy; he had died of pneumonia in prison; he had escaped to France. Young Paco, the blond dynamiter of enemy tanks, was still a local fisherman — you could run into him at any time; no, he had blown himself up; he had married and gone to Majorca.

Extract from As I Walked Out One Midsummer Morning by Laurie Lee

SENTENCE PATTERNS

Punctuation is not the only method of structuring sentences. Many sentences depend for their effect on the order in which their component parts are placed.

(i) *Inversion*

In English, the normal order is for the subject to come first, followed by the words which tell us more about the subject (the predicate).

Flames leapt up and up.

However, occasionally, this order is reversed:

Up and up leapt the flames.

Here the predicate comes *before* the subject. This technique, where the subject is delayed, is known as *inversion* and can be used to alter the emphasis in a sentence.

In his poem *Church Going,* Philip Larkin recalls visiting a rather dull suburban church with the words "Yet stop I did". The inversion is much more forceful than the normal word order which would be "Yet I did stop".

Inversion tends to be used in shorter sentences in order to place the emphasis on a particular word. In longer sentences, however, there are numerous other methods which a writer can employ to stress a particular part.

(ii) *Repetition*

A writer may decide to repeat certain word patterns to achieve a particular purpose. During the Second World War, the Prime Minister, Winston Churchill, broadcast many speeches on the radio. One of the techniques he used very skilfully was repetition, as in the famous speech delivered after the evacuation of Dunkirk in 1940:

> We shall fight on the beaches, we shall fight on the landing grounds, we shall fight in the fields and in the streets, we shall fight in the hills. We shall never surrender.

The series of repeated statements beginning "we shall fight . . ." is effective in inspiring his listeners never to give up on their efforts.

(iii) *Climax and Anti-climax*

A closer look at Churchill's sentence shows that there is a deliberate order to the places listed. The speaker is tracing the progress of the enemy troops from landing on the beaches, through the countryside, to the towns and to the higher ground beyond and saying that they would meet with resistance at every stage. The whole list builds up to the last sentence which has greater impact because it is so short: "We shall never surrender". Placing a number of items in ascending order like this, with the most important being kept to the last, is called *climax*.

The opposite effect — when the author builds up to something which does not in fact come — is *anti-climax*.

> She crept downstairs, taking infinite care to avoid the loose steps which she knew would creak. Her fingers trembled as they felt for the light switch. Slowly, she pushed open the door, not knowing what to expect. The room was completely empty.

(iv) *Antithesis*

Another way of arranging ideas within a sentence is to balance opposites together to create a contrast, a technique called *antithesis*. In the poem *An Irish Airman foresees his Death* by W.B. Yeats, the pilot wonders why he is taking part in the war:

> Those that I fight I do not hate
> Those that I guard I do not love.

Antithesis is particularly suited to poetry because its effect can be reinforced by the poem's rhythm, as in the above example. But the technique is often used in prose as well. Journalists trying to persuade their readers and politicians delivering speeches often use antithesis to state a point in a memorable way. Often, the politician hopes that the journalist will find his comment "quotable" so that it will find its way into the next day's headlines. Towards the end of his 1961 Inauguration Address, President John F. Kennedy said:

> My fellow Americans, ask not what your country can do for you; ask what you can do for your country.

Kennedy was aiming to make an impressive and statesmanlike impact here, but antithesis can equally well have a humorous effect. Scottish comedian Robbie Coltrane recently published an account of his travels across America in a 1950s convertible, entitled *Coltrane in a Cadillac*. After talking to the owner of a gun shop in Dodge City, Kansas, he observed that:

> You can take the American out of the OK Corral, but you can't take the OK Corral out of the American.

(v) *Long and Short Sentences*

We have looked at how the techniques of repetition, climax and antithesis can be used within single sentences. Similar effects can also be obtained with a series of sentences in a paragraph. A piece of writing in which all the sentences are of a similar length or follow the same grammatical pattern will be dull and lifeless to read. A good writer knows instinctively when to balance a long sentence with a short one.

Example 1

In this extract from a short story called *The Followers* by the Welsh poet Dylan Thomas, different sentence lengths are used to speed up and slow down the narrative:

> We ran up the gravel drive, and around the corner of the house, and into the avenue and out onto St Augustus Crescent. The rain roared down to drown the town. There we stopped for breath. We did not speak or look at each other. Then we walked through the rain. At Victoria Corner, we stopped again.

The first sentence conveys a feeling of speed and continuous movement by using the simple conjunction "and" three times. This contrasts effectively with the short statement: "There we stopped for breath." The slower, interrupted progress of the characters in the rest of the paragraph is conveyed by a series of short sentences.

Example 2

In the following descriptive passage from E. M. Forster's novel *A Room with a View,* the author alternates between short and long passages:

> Miss Bartlett not favouring the scheme, they walked up the hill in a silence which was only broken by the rector naming some fern. On the summit they paused. The sky had grown wilder since he stood there last hour, giving to the land a tragic greatness that is rare in Surrey. Grey clouds were charging across tissues of white, which stretched and shredded and tore slowly, until through their final layers there gleamed a hint of the disappearing blue. Summer was retreating.

Why do you think Forster has placed the two statements "On the summit they paused" and "Summer was retreating" as separate short sentences on their own? Try rewriting the passage punctuating it differently and observe whether the description becomes less effective.

WHAT THE EXAMINER IS LOOKING FOR

You should now be able to identify different types of sentences; understand how punctuation is used to clarify the structure; recognise techniques such as repetition, climax and antithesis; and observe why authors use varied sentence lengths. (This knowledge will also be useful for your Review of Personal Reading. If you have chosen a prose work for this, try to identify how the writer uses some of the techniques discussed in this section.)

> REMEMBER: a question on sentence structure does not want you to explain what the writer means. It is asking you to comment on *how the sentence is put together.*

FOR PRACTICE

For each of the following extracts, answer the question

> *Comment on the sentence structure . . .*

Once you have identified features of the sentence structure, go on to explain what you think the writer achieves by using these techniques. Don't make vague comments like "this is effective" or "the writer uses repetition for emphasis". You must say "this is effective *because* . . ." or "the writer uses repetition to emphasise that . . .".

1. Let every nation know, whether it wishes us well or ill, that we shall pay any price, bear any burden, meet any hardship, support any friend, oppose any foe to assure the survival and success of liberty.

2. The second and the third day passed, and still my tormentor came not. Once again I breathed as a free man. The monster, in terror, had fled the premises for ever! I should behold it no more! My happiness was supreme!

3. "Had you rather Caesar were living and die all slaves, than that Caesar were dead, to live all free men? As Caesar loved me, I weep for him; as he was fortunate, I rejoice at it; as he was valiant, I honour him; but, as he was ambitious, I slew him."

4. If my books had been any worse, I should not have been invited to Hollywood, and if they had been any better, I should not have come.

5. I often played in the back courts at Shettleston with Johnny and Joe, one of several pairs of inseparables in my class at Eastbank. We played at tig and jumped from the wash-houses, but it was something different that kept them playing there when we might have been somewhere else. They refused to tell me what it was, but they kept hinting about it, and often with the undertone of dispute. I asked them what the secret was, but the one thing they agreed on was that nobody else could ever know about it. Then Johnny told me when Joe wasn't there. It was a girl.

    Extract from *Dancing in the Streets* by Clifford Hanley

6. Fog everywhere. Fog up the river, where it flows among green airs and meadows; fog down the river, where it rolls defiled among the tiers of shipping, and the waterside pollutions of a great (and dirty) city. Fog on the Essex marshes, fog on the Kentish heights. Fog creeping into the cabooses of collier-brigs; fog lying out on the yards, and hovering in the rigging of great ships; fog drooping on the gunwales of barges and small boats.

7. With mother I was beyond reason. I continually criticised her, corrected her and quarrelled with her every day. I even threw her own china at her.

8. With this faith we will be able to work together, to pray together, to struggle together, to go to jail together, to climb up for freedom together, knowing that we will be free one day.

9. Walter Scott was generous. But he was prudent too. Anxious to secure comfort for his family — he now had four children — he invested his savings in Ballantyne's printing business. Thus he became a partner in a venture which might have been successful but for two factors: Ballantyne's inability to size up a business situation, and Scott's inability to size up Ballantyne.

10. In they all came, one after another: some shyly, some boldly, some gracefully, some awkwardly, some pushing, some pulling; in they all came, anyhow and everyhow. Away they all went, twenty couples at once: hands half round and back again the other way; down the middle and up again; round and round in various stages of affectionate grouping; old top couple always turning up in the wrong place; new top couple starting off again, as soon as they got there; all top couples at last and not a bottom one to help them.

(There are more examples for practice in analysing sentence structure questions at the end of Appendix I: Grammar and Syntax).

Checklist for tackling structure questions

✳ Can you identify the type of sentence: statement, question, exclamation, command, minor sentence?

✳ Does the writer use rhetorical questions?

✳ How is punctuation used to divide up the sentence?

✳ Do you notice anything about the order of the words: inversion? climax? anti-climax?

✳ Is there an element of balance between different parts of the sentence?

✳ Does the author vary the lengths of his sentences?

✳ Is parenthesis used?

VARIETIES OF LANGUAGE

Comment on the word choice of . . .

Before you can answer individual questions on the language of a passage of writing, you need to establish whether it is written in a *formal* or an *informal* style and whether the word choice is *literal* or *figurative*. By the end of this section you should have a clear understanding of these terms.

Formal and Informal Language

It is possible to convey the same piece of information in very different styles of language. The list of by-laws for a Tennis Club might state that:

> Members may introduce, with the prior approval of a designated Committee member, not more than one visitor at a time, but the names of the introducing member and visitor must be recorded on the Visitors' sheet on the club notice board on each occasion. Failure to do this will result in the withdrawal of this privilege from the member concerned.

On the other hand, if the Club President sees a player disregarding the rule, he might say:

> If you don't write your names on the notice board, you'll not be allowed to bring your friend again.

The basic meaning is the same in both cases but the language of the first is very formal while the second is informal. What are the differences between the two?

FORMAL LANGUAGE	INFORMAL LANGUAGE
Usually written	Usually spoken, or at least a written version of conversational/colloquial expressions
No abbreviations	Uses shortened forms
Grammatically correct	May use looser sentence structures
Wider range of word choice, including complex or technical vocabulary	More common, everyday words, some perhaps being non-standard English
Impersonal tone (author may put his own feelings aside and adopt a balanced and unbiased stance, i.e. *objective*)	Personal approach (using first person "I" and second person "you"), i.e. *subjective*
Tends to be factual	May include feelings

Within the general division into formal/informal language, there are a number of other related terms that you should know.

Jargon is a specialised type of formal language which includes technical terms relating to a particular subject or occupation. For instance, terms such as *byte*, *icon*, *dialogue box*, *file menu*, *monitor* and *font* belong to the jargon of computing. Clearly, the expert needs to use such vocabulary in the course of his work or studies. The term jargon, however, can also have negative associations, and is sometimes used to describe the use of unnecessarily complex and pompous words which may in reality be no more than a way of making something obvious sound impressive. This amusing example of a conversation between a probation officer and a judge was quoted in the correspondence column of a recent newspaper:

Probation report: He hails from a multi-delinquent family with a high incarceration index.

Judge: You mean the whole lot are inside?

Probation report: Inter-sibling rivalry hindered his ongoing relationships making him an isolate in a stress situation with his peers.

Judge: You mean that he hated his brothers?

Rhetorical language is another aspect of formal English. Such language aims to give an elevated, dignified and impressive effect and is most often used in the course of a formal speech, such as a politician addressing a conference. (In fact, the word "rhetoric" means the art of public speaking). A favourite technique used by such speakers is to phrase a statement in the form of a question (**rhetorical question**). The speaker is not really asking the audience to answer and the listeners already know what the speaker's answer would be:

Shall we relax our efforts at the very moment when victory is in our grasp?

For a longer example of rhetorical language, see the extract from the speech by Hillary Clinton on pages 83 and 84.

Dialect and slang: At the other end of the linguistic spectrum, dialect and slang are particular varieties of informal/conversational language. Dialect refers to a way of speaking in a town or district whereas slang involves the use of non-standard conversational word choice. If you have read *Sunset Song* you will be familiar with Lewis Grassic Gibbon's use of dialect. More recently, William McIlvanney, in novels such as *Docherty*, has attempted to put conversational dialect into a written form to give a more authentic feel to the dialogue:

Ah'm sorry Ah hiv tae turn ye doon. Ye're guid but ye're auld, son.

Michael Munro has made an in-depth study of Glasgow "patter" and has collected enough examples of it to fill two books, *The Patter* (1985) and *The Patter, Another Blast* (1988). He believes that dialect develops because it is "a common form of identity". "For the homesick it is a concrete link with home. It is the medium for shared humour, remembered songs and poems, catch-phrases, and greetings that will always identify you more truly than any passport photograph."

FOR PRACTICE

In the following extract from James Herriot's *Vet in a Spin* , a woman finally decides to bring her dog to the vet for treatment after her husband has tried all kinds of home-made remedies. Identify how the passage combines *(a)* informal conversational language *(b)* dialect and *(c)* jargon.

'Just look at me good dog, Mr Herriot!' She rapped out.

I looked. 'Good heavens!' I gasped.

The little animal was almost completely bald. His skin was dry, scaly and wrinkled, and his head hung down as though he were under sedation.

'Aye, you're surprised, aren't you?' she barked. 'He's in a terrible state, isn't he?'

'I'm afraid so. I wouldn't have known him.'

'No, nobody would. Ah think the world o' this dog and just look at 'im!' She paused and snorted a few times. 'And I know who's responsible, don't you?'

'Well . . .'

'Oh, you do. It's that husband o' mine.' She paused and glared at me, breathing rapidly. 'What d'you think of my husband, Mr Herriot?'

'I really don't know him very well. I . . . '

'Well, ah know 'im and he's a gawp. He's a great gawp. Knows everything and knows nowt. He's played around wi' me good dog till he's ruined 'im.'

I didn't say anything. I was studying the keeshound. It was the first time I had been able to observe him closely and I was certain I knew the cause of his trouble.

Mrs Pilling stuck her jaw out further and continued.

'First me husband said it was eczema. Is it?'

'No.'

'Then 'e said it was mange. Is it?'

'No.'

'D'you know what it is?'

'Yes.'

'Well, will you tell me please?'

'It's myxoedema.'

'Myx . . .?'

'Wait a minute,' I said. 'I'll just make absolutely sure.' I reached for my stethoscope and put it on the dog's chest. And the bradycardia was there as I expected, the slow, slow heartbeat of hypothyroidism. 'Yes, that's it. Not a shadow of a doubt about it.'

'What did you call it?'

'Myxoedema. It's a thyroid deficiency — there's a gland in his neck which isn't doing its job properly.'

'And that makes 'is hair fall out?'

'Oh yes. And it also causes this typical scaliness and wrinkling of the skin.'

'Aye, but he's half asleep all t'time. How about that?'

'Another classical symptom. Dogs with this condition become very lethargic — lose all their energy.'

She reached out and touched the dog's skin, bare and leathery where once the coat had grown in bushy glory. 'And can you cure it?'

'Yes.'

'Now Mr Herriot, don't take this the wrong way, but could you be mistaken? Are ye positive it's this myxi-whatever-it-is?'

'Of course I am. It's a straightforward case.'

'Straightforward to you, maybe.' She flushed and appeared to be grinding her teeth. 'But not straightforward to that clever husband o' mine. The great lubbert! When ah think what he's put me good dog through — ah could kill 'im.'

Extract from *Vet in a Spin* by James Herriot

FOR DISCUSSION: Divide a sheet of paper into three columns, headed Dialect, Informal English and Formal English.

Working in pairs, write down in the first column a list of local expressions that you are familiar with.

Then try to "translate" these into standard conversational English and, if possible, a very formal style of making the same point.

Which of the three is most effective in each case? Does stating a point in a certain way make it more humorous?

Literal and Figurative Language

Although the Tennis Club rules, the probation report and the story about the vet vary widely in their degree of formality, all are examples of language being used to convey information in a *literal* way. This just means that words are being used to mean exactly what they say: their use corresponds to the definitions you would find if you looked them up in a dictionary.

Obviously, most language is used in this sense, but words can also be used in a non-literal way. In everyday conversation we use expressions like these:

> She's only trying to wind you up — don't rise to the bait!
> Keep practising — maybe you'll be a big star one day!

Here the physical objects ("bait", "star") are not actually the real subject of discussion but are brought in by way of comparison. These words are being used *figuratively* or *metaphorically*.

> *REMEMBER*: A simple way of working out whether a word is being used literally or figuratively is to ask whether the thing is actually physically present, or whether it is brought in by way of comparison.

FOR PRACTICE

Look back at the first four samples of writing to be found on pages 18 and 19 in the section on "Tackling Structure Questions". With a partner, discuss the word choice of these passages and work out where words are being used literally and where they are being used figuratively.

(a) *Figures of speech involving comparisons*

There are many different kinds of figurative language — often called *figures of speech* — and you will already have met some of these, perhaps in the course of studying poetry. In tackling the Textual Analysis part of the Higher Paper, knowledge of these terms is essential. Three in particular attempt to paint a clearer picture of what something looks like by comparing it to another object that the reader might be able to visualise more easily:

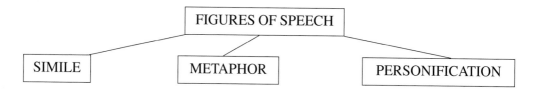

Simile:

A comparison in which one thing is said to be like something else (A is like B). Laurie Lee uses the following simile to describe how passers-by reacted when he played his violin in the street for the first time:

> It was as though the note of the fiddle touched some sub-conscious nerve that had to be answered — like a baby's cry.
>
> Extract from *As I Walked Out One Midsummer Morning* by Laurie Lee

The sound of the "note of the fiddle" is the real subject; the "baby's cry" is not actually heard but is brought in as a comparison. A baby's scream cannot be ignored; in the same way, the pedestrians felt compelled to react to the music.

Note, however, that not every comparison with the word "like" or "as" in it is necessarily a figurative use of language: "The scenery of Ireland is like the Highlands of Scotland" is not really a simile as it is simply a comparison between two similar, literal subjects.

Metaphor:

Here the word "like" or "as" is missed out in the comparison. The subject is said to be the same as the figurative comparison (A is B). On his travels in Spain, Laurie Lee met an attractive girl who was a fanatical communist. He uses the following metaphor to describe her:

> Her lovely mouth was a political megaphone.

Again, her mouth is the real subject and the "political megaphone" is brought in as a comparison to emphasise, not just that she talks non-stop about politics, but that she does so in a loud and perhaps aggressive way.

Writers sometimes sustain and develop the one comparison over several lines. Here a journalist is discussing the subject of a single European currency:

> Europe is an express train heading for monetary union. But a train can come off the rails. Last week we were being urged to take our seats in the dining-car. We should have been just in time for the signalmen's errors in France and Germany. The row on the footplate was set off by the German finance minister . . .

This technique is known as an **extended metaphor**. The initial metaphor of the express train is continued in the sentences which follow by references to other words connected with railways, such as "dining car", "signalman" and "footplate".

Personification:

A special type of metaphor in which an inanimate object is given human characteristics, moods, reactions and so on. This figure of speech is often used in descriptions of nature, as in Tennyson's poem *The Lady of Shalott* :

> The broad stream in his banks complaining

A river cannot really "complain": the personification is used to indicate that the water seemed noisy, restless and turbulent as if it felt dissatisfied.

As these examples would suggest, figurative language is used in literature to help readers picture more clearly the subject being described. *Imagery* is a general term for any language techniques which paint pictures in words by making comparisons and covers specific figures of speech like simile, metaphor, personification and so on.

WHAT THE EXAMINER IS LOOKING FOR

A previous Higher Interpretation passage was on the subject of burying nuclear waste. Referring to a sentence which read,

> How, then, should the rulers of today warn future generations of the filthy brew that they have buried beneath their feet?

candidates were asked to:

> Explain how effective you find the metaphor "filthy brew".
>
> **2 marks**

In tackling such questions, ask yourself

✳   What is being compared to what?

✳   In what respects are the two similar?

✳   How does the comparison help you to visualise the subject better?

Here are the steps by which you could arrive at a good answer for the question in the box above:

✳   A store of nuclear waste is being compared to the disgusting concoction in a witch's cauldron.

✳   Both are mixtures of unpleasant ingredients which are extremely harmful to man.

✳   The metaphor helps you appreciate the unpleasant and harmful nature of the waste.

Having clarified these three points in your mind, you can now devise a well-worded answer:

Answer: The metaphor is very effective as "brew" has connotations of a poisonous concoction in a witch's cauldron, made of disgusting ingredients. "Filthy" strengthens the sense of its revolting and disgusting nature. The metaphor helps the reader appreciate the unpleasant and harmful nature of the waste and its potential for having evil consequences for man.

FOR PRACTICE

Bearing in mind the advice given on the previous pages, comment on the effectiveness of the imagery in the following examples:

1. A house like this became a dinosaur, occupying too much ground and demanding to be fed new sinks and drainpipes and a sea of electricity. Such a house became a fossil, stranded among neighbours long since chopped up into flats and bed-sitting rooms.

    Extract from *The House in Norham Gardens* by Penelope Lively

2. The shipyard cranes have come down again
    To drink at the river, turning their long necks
    And saying to their reflections on the Clyde,
    "How noble we are."

    Extract from [Poem] *Landscape with One Figure* by Douglas Dunn

3. The gas-mantle putted like a sick man's heart. Dimmed to a bead of light, it made the room mysterious as a chapel. The polished furniture, enriched by darkness, entombed fragments of the firelight that moved like tapers in a tunnel. The brasses glowed like icons.

    Extract from *Docherty* by William McIlvanney

4. But pleasures are like poppies spread:
    You seize the flow'r, its bloom is shed;
    Or like the snow falls in the river,
    A moment white — then melts for ever.

5. My instructor, one of Seville's most respected professors of the guitar, was a small, sad man, exquisitely polite and patient. Each day, at the stroke of ten, he knocked softly at my door and entered on tiptoe, as though into a sick room, carrying his guitar-case like a doctor's bag.
    "How are we today?" he would ask sympathetically, "and how do we proceed?"
    After an hour's examination, during which he tested all my faulty co-ordinations, he would hand me a page of exercises and bid me take them twice a day.

    Extract from *As I Walked Out One Midsummer Morning* by Laurie Lee

6. Built like a gorilla but less timid . . .
    he walks the sidewalk and the
    thin tissue over violence.

    Extract from poem *Brooklyn Cop* by Norman MacCaig

7. At the open window of the great library of Blandings Castle, drooping like a wet sock as was his habit when he had nothing to prop his spine against, the Earl of Emsworth, that amiable and bone-headed peer, stood gazing out over his domain.

    Extract from *Leave it to Psmith* by P.G. Wodehouse

8. *Here, R.L. Stevenson is describing an attack on an antique shop dealer.*

"This, perhaps may suit," observed the dealer and then, as he began to re-arise, Markheim bounded from behind upon his victim. The long, skewer-like dagger flashed and fell. The dealer struggled like a hen, striking his temple on the shelf, and then tumbled to the floor in a heap . . . In those poor miserly clothes, in that ungainly attitude, the dealer lay like so much sawdust.

9. The rain raced along horizontally, sticking into them like glass splinters till they were wet through.

10. Time, the great magician, had wrought much here.

Extracts from Tess of the D'Urbervilles by Thomas Hardy

(b)   *Other useful figures of speech and literary terms*

There are many other literary techniques which can loosely be classified as **figures of speech**. This term can include almost any use of language to achieve some kind of special effect beyond the basic function of conveying information. Some of these figures of speech relate more to the sound of the word than to its meaning, which is why such techniques are often to be found in poetry; other figures of speech have to do with exaggeration. It would probably be safe to say that what they all have in common is that the writer's main concern is less with the straightforward literal meaning of the words than with the achievement of a particular effect. The effect might be descriptive, or humorous, or sarcastic, or emphatic, and so on.

The following list of definitions will be useful for reference and will help you to answer interpretation questions like

> *Comment on the effectiveness of . . .*
> *Comment on the tone of . . .*

Although it is not absolutely necessary to know *all* of these terms, you will find that it is often simpler to identify a technique by its proper name rather than struggling to explain it in another way. For convenience, these terms have been grouped into four categories:

(i)   ***Sound effects***
   Alliteration: This is usually defined as a series of words in which the same letter is repeated, usually at the beginning of two or more words. However, remember that, as with all literary techniques, the writer must be using it to create a particular effect. Once they have been introduced to the idea of alliteration, students sometimes start to find examples of it everywhere! As there are only 26 letters in the alphabet, it is

inevitable that in some sentences there will be some words with the same initial letter:

> He carried a box of books up to the storeroom on the top floor of the building.

There are three words beginning with "b" here but all of them are simple nouns and there does not appear to be any particular literary effect intended. However, when the travel writer Patrick Leigh-Fermor, describing a town in Holland, talks about the

> clip-clop of clogs on the cobblestones

the alliteration is clearly deliberate: you can almost hear the rhythmical sound of the wooden shoes on the street.

Onomatopoeia is a name given to words which imitate the sound they are describing and you may have noticed that this figure of speech often works in conjunction with alliteration. As in the above quotation, alliteration helps to create an onomatopoeic effect. This is how D.H. Lawrence describes a snake drinking from a water trough in his poem *Snake*:

> He sipped with his straight mouth,
> Softly drank through his straight gums, into his slack long body,
> Silently.

The alliteration of the letter "s" (also known as **sibilance**) creates a "hissing" effect appropriate to a description of a snake.

Pun: a play on words involving words which sound similar but have different meanings. The effect intended is usually a humorous one, although there are plenty of bad jokes that depend on puns!

> "Waiter!"
> "Yes sir?"
> "What's this supposed to be?"
> "It's bean soup, sir."
> "I don't care what it's been. What is it now?"

(ii) *Overstating, understating and talking in circles*

Hyperbole is deliberate exaggeration in order to emphasise the point being made — often for a humorous effect. The television presenter Clive James often uses this technique with great skill. He describes Marlon Brando as "Hollywood's number one broody outcast" and says that:

> He could order a cheeseburger with fries and make it sound like a challenge to the Establishment.

Extract from *Fame in the Twentieth Century* by Clive James

Litotes is the opposite of hyperbole: deliberate understatement. In *My Family and Other Animals*, Gerald Durrell writes of his mother:

> On Monday morning I found her in the garage being pursued round and round by an irate pelican which she was trying to feed with sardines from a tin.
>
> "I'm glad you've come, dear," she panted; "this pelican is a little difficult to handle."

As with so many other figures of speech, hyperbole and litotes are not confined to writing but are often used in everyday conversation:

Isn't there anything to drink? I'm dying of thirst! (Hyperbole)

The teacher wasn't exactly overjoyed when I told her that I'd left my work at home. (Litotes)

Euphemism: a way of making an unwelcome truth seem less harsh or unpleasant by dressing it up in inoffensive language. Many euphemisms are connected with the subject of death, as when we say that someone has "passed away" rather than "died". In 1948, the novelist Evelyn Waugh wrote a novel called *The Loved One* which makes fun of American funeral customs, in the course of which he uses many euphemisms such as "leave-taking", "Slumber Room", "Whispering Glades" and "Before Need Provision Arrangements". Can you guess what some of these terms might refer to?

Euphemisms are equally plentiful in the world of politics. One of the most famous examples came from the 1950s Prime Minister, Sir Anthony Eden, who once said: "We are not at war with Egypt. We are in a state of armed conflict."

Circumlocution: this literally means "to talk round" something — in other words, to state something in a long, roundabout way rather than addressing the subject simply and directly. The nineteenth-century novelist Charles Dickens poked fun at lawyers and government officials for doing this (see page 49).

(iii) *Contrasts, opposites and contradictions*

Paradox: a statement which appears to be a contradiction but which, on closer examination, does contain a truth. For example, *to preserve the peace, prepare for war* seems to be a contradiction, but it is based on the "deterrent" idea that if one side builds up its military strength then the enemy will not dare to attack, and thus peace will be maintained. The oft-quoted comment by Oscar Wilde is an example of paradox: "Nowadays people know the price of everything, and the value of nothing."

Oxymoron: a condensed form of paradox, in which two opposites are placed side by side to heighten the effect of contrast. Edwin Muir's poem *The Horses* ends with horses coming to a group of human survivors of a nuclear war and voluntarily allowing themselves to be used to plough the land: the poet describes their action as "free servitude". (If this poem is in your poetry book, read it and try to work out the significance of this oxymoron.)

Juxtaposition simply means placing side by side. In the above example of oxymoron, it could be said that the two opposites are placed in juxtaposition. A writer might deliberately place two sentences beside each other to highlight the contrast between them. Here is another example from Clive James' book on *Fame*:

> Dustin Hoffman became famous in the sixties in *The Graduate* playing a nervous young man who suspected that life in America was stacked against him. In the seventies he became more famous still as an even more nervous, slightly less young man, who *knew* that life in America was stacked against him.

(iv) *The new, the old and the overused*

Neologism: Coining of a new word, usually to describe a recent development or invention for which an appropriate term does not exist. Some modern examples are: microwave oven, filofax, teletext, video-conferencing.

Archaism: Whereas a neologism is a newly-invented word, an archaism denotes a word from the past which is no longer in current use.

> Arm thyself lightly, mount to horse, keep thy land, aid thy men, hurtle into the press. Thou needest not to strike another, neither to be smitten down.

A writer may deliberately try to write in an archaic style in an attempt to recapture the feel of a historical period.

Cliché: an expression which at one time might have been original but has now become overused, such as "in this day and age" or "all part and parcel of". Well-worn similes like "as white as snow" are clichés and should be avoided like the plague (another cliché!).

FOR PRACTICE

Working in pairs, identify which of the above techniques are used in the following extracts. Remember that more than one technique might be used in each case.

You should then go on to consider the more difficult question of *why* the writer has used that technique. What effect is he trying to achieve?

1. We wait, listening
    to bus tyres on rain say "hush" and "west".

    Extract from poem *Aunt Janet's Museum* by Kathleen Jamie

2. Ben Battle was a soldier bold,
    And used to life's alarms.
    A cannonball shot off his legs
    So he laid down his arms.

3. We come across crowds and confetti, weddings
    With well-wishers, relatives, whimsical bridesmaids.

    Extract from poem *Arrangements* by Douglas Dunn

4. The machine sobs
    through its cycle. The rhythm throbs
    and changes. Suds drool and slobber in the churn.

    Extract from poem *Laundrette* by Liz Lochead

5. It was a morning of mysterious monotones: black rocks above and a black sea beneath.

Extract from *As I Walked Out One Midsummer Morning* by Laurie Lee

6. Christmas found me
   With other fond and foolish girls
   at the menswear counters
   Shopping for the ties that bind.

Extract from poem *Obituary* by Liz Lochhead

7. [He] goes off . . . leaving behind only
   books that will not be read
   and fruitless fruits.

From Norman MacCaig's poem about
a visit to a dying patient in hospital.

8. He started off as an Olympic swimmer who won so many medals he could stay fit just carrying them around.

From Clive James' description of Johnny Weismuller,
the actor who became famous in the role of Tarzan.

9. *Member of Parliament:* Is the government still intent on implementing these savage cuts which will strike at the very fabric of our society?
   Government Minister: We are carrying out an in-depth examination of current expenditure to see if economies can be made which will ultimately benefit the taxpayer.

10. "I have our brochure here setting out our services. Were you thinking of interment or incineration?"
    "Pardon me?"
    "Buried or burned?"

Extract from *The Loved One* by Evelyn Waugh

11. "I would speak with you, Sir Minstrel," said the young knight. "If thou dost not find the air of this morning too harsh, heartily do I wish thou wouldst fairly tell me what can have induced thee, being, as thou seemest, a man of sense, to thrust thyself into a wild country like this, at such a time."

12. It was a game of two halves. United set out their stall to soak up Rovers' pressure and hit on the break; however, they flirted with disaster and only a crunching tackle by Alan Gough on Marc Laudrup as the latter was about to pull the trigger kept the scores level. Towards the interval, Rovers did score twice through Tommy Shearer, leaving United a mountain to climb and giving themselves a valuable cushion.

In the second half it all went pear-shaped for Rovers: Kevin Durie scored two fine goals to throw United a lifeline. United manager, Walter Jansen, was over the moon while his counterpart, Roy McLean, declared himself sick as a parrot. This was British football at its worst.

13. Given the nature of the hotel I'd expected the menu to feature items like brown windsor soup and roast beef and Yorkshire pudding, but of course things have moved on in the hotel trade. The menu now was richly endowed with ten-guinea words that you wouldn't have seen on a menu ten years ago — "noisettes", "tartare", "duxelle", "coulis", "timbale" — and written in a curious inflated language with eccentric capitalizations. I had, and I quote, "Fanned Galia Melon and Cumbrian Air Dried Ham served with a Mixed leaf Salad" followed by "Fillet Steak served with a crushed Black Peppercorn Sauce flamed in Brandy and finished with Cream", which together were nearly as pleasurable to read as to eat.

I was greatly taken with this new way of talking and derived considerable pleasure from speaking it to the waiter. I asked him for a lustre of water freshly drawn from the house tap and presented *au nature* in a cylinder of glass, and when he came round with the bread rolls I entreated him to present me a tongued rondel of blanched wheat oven baked and masked in a poppy-seed coating. I was just getting warmed up to this and about to ask for a fanned lap coverlet, freshly laundered and scented with a delicate hint of Omo, to replace the one that had slipped from my lap and now lay recumbent on the horizontal walking surface anterior to my feet when he handed me a card that said "Sweets Menu" and I realized that we were back in the no-nonsense world of English.

Extract from *Notes from a Small Island* © Bill Bryson, 1995

TONE

Most people find interpretation questions on tone very difficult to answer — mainly because they don't really understand what is being asked for.

> *Comment on the tone of . . .*
>
> **1 mark**

Tone does not relate directly to meaning but rather to *the way in which something is said*. It refers to a particular attitude or feeling conveyed by the writer.

Consider a simple question like:

Where have you been?

These words could be spoken in various situations:

    ✳   by someone talking to a friend who has recently been on holiday
    ✳   by someone talking to a friend who has not been seen for a long time
    ✳   by a parent to a teenage son or daughter who arrives home at 4 a.m.

Exactly the same words might be used but they would be said in quite different ways. This is what is meant by *tone*.

Try it yourself

In pairs, try reading the question aloud as you feel it might be said in order to convey a particular attitude or emotion on the part of the speaker. Your partner should try to guess what tone you are adopting. You might try to express anger, surprise, sarcasm, resentment, mockery, bewilderment and so on. You can then try the same exercise with one or two more simple sentences you have made up yourselves.

In speech, the tone of voice used would make the speaker's feelings clear. In writing, however, you must look at the word choice to find clues to the feelings or attitude of the author.

Serious or Humorous?

It would be impossible to list every nuance of tone that a writer might use, as there are as many as there are attitudes. But they can be broadly categorised. You must first consider whether the author is being serious or light-hearted about his subject.

If he is being light-hearted, the tone may be **humorous** in a straightforward way, where the author is finding his subject funny and he hopes his reader will too.

A **flippant** tone is where the author is showing an irreverent attitude to something normally taken seriously. An example is to be found in Philip Larkin's poem *Church Going*, where the poet enters a church and describes the altar thus: "some brass and stuff, up at the holy end." Here the use of colloquial and informal expressions conveys his lack of respect.

A light-hearted tone will often include **informal** and **conversational** language, whereas a serious, respectful tone will use more formal words.

The word **conversational** itself can describe a tone, particularly a **chatty, friendly** tone, as if the writer is confiding in a friend. An example is the narrative tone in the opening chapter of *Sunset Song* by Lewis Grassic Gibbon, where the writer is gossiping to his readers about his characters:

> "Chae . . . wasn't the quarrelsome kind except when roused, so he was well-liked, though folk laughed at him. But God knows, who is it they don't laugh at?"

An enthusiastic **effusive** tone might be used in an advertisement to persuade someone to buy something. A list of gushing superlatives would be an example of this.

Irony is the name given to the figure of speech where an author says the opposite of what he really means. This could be purely for humorous effect, but there is often a serious purpose behind irony. An author's feelings can be expressed more forcefully for being inverted in this way. (The writer Jane Austen is famous for her use of irony, and there is a good example of this in the interpretation passage on Novels on pages 87 and 88.)

A **tongue-in-cheek** tone is a form of irony: the writer will *sound* serious, but there will be a sense of ridicule behind this. **Euphemism** is a common feature of this tone. An example might be the expression "tired and emotional" to mean "drunk" which the satirical magazine *Private Eye* uses to avoid lawsuits from the prominent people whom it exposes.

A **satirical** tone is an extreme form of irony. Here a writer is funny in a more savage way : he holds a subject up to ridicule in order to attack it. This is the tone adopted by George Orwell in *Animal Farm*, for example, where he satirised Russian Communists by comparing them to pigs. The satirist's purpose is deeply serious although on the surface he may appear light-hearted.

A **serious** tone is obviously used for serious purposes, on solemn occasions: a funeral speech, for example. Words such as **formal**, **ponderous** or even **pompous** might be applied.

Focus on Irony

Irony is one of the most common techniques used to convey tone. As was explained before, the most common form of irony is when someone says the *opposite* of what they really mean. If a friend were to say at the end of the summer holidays, "I can't wait to get back to school!", this would presumably be an example of irony.

A famous example of this kind of irony in literature can be found in Shakespeare's *Julius Caesar*. After Caesar has been assassinated, his right-hand man, Antony, is permitted by Brutus (one of the leaders of the conspiracy against Caesar) to make a speech to the people of Rome. Brutus allows Antony to do this on condition that he does not criticise the conspirators but Antony cleverly uses irony to make his point, attacking Brutus while apparently praising him:

> When that the poor have cried, Caesar hath wept:
> Ambition should be made of sterner stuff:
> Yet Brutus says he was ambitious;
> And Brutus is an honourable man.

FOR PRACTICE

In his novel Little Dorrit, *Charles Dickens makes fun of officials and bureaucrats who get tied up in form-filling and generate more and more administrative paper-work. He invents an imaginary government department which has turned the creation of unnecessary "red tape" into an art form and calls it the "Circumlocution Office". (Look back at page 43 to see why Dickens chose this title.)*

Identify which parts of the following extract are ironic. How can you tell? What effect is produced?

> The Circumlocution Office was (as everybody knows without being told) the most important Department under Government. No public business of any kind could possibly be done at any time, without the acquiescence of the Circumlocution Office. If another Gunpowder Plot had been discovered half an hour before the lighting of the match, nobody would have been justified in saving the parliament until there had been half a score of boards, half a bushel of minutes, several sacks of official memoranda, and a family-vault full of ungrammatical correspondence, on the part of the Circumlocution Office.
>
> This glorious establishment had been early in the field, when the one sublime principle involving the difficult art of governing a country, was first distinctly revealed to statesmen. It had been foremost to study that bright revelation, and

Continued on next page

to carry its shining influence through the whole of the official proceedings. Whatever was required to be done, the Circumlocution Office was beforehand with all the public departments in the art of perceiving — HOW NOT TO DO IT.

Through this delicate perception, through the tact with which it invariably seized it, and through the genius with which it always acted on it, the Circumlocution Office had risen to overtop all the public departments . . .

Emotive language

For serious purposes, an **emotive** tone is often used. As the name implies, this aims at stirring up emotions in the reader, by shocking, angering or disturbing him. This is done by using words or expressions expressing extreme emotions.

This example was written by a sports journalist criticising the tension at a Rangers/Celtic football match:

> Nowhere else on the planet do footballers perform in front of vast crowds so full of bile, hatred and bigotry. I have yet to find another place on the planet where a sporting occasion includes a ritual singing of some ditty celebrating a distant battle which took place 307 years ago.
>
> © *The Mail on Sunday* 9.11.97

Here the writer uses **repetition**, and **hyperbole**: "on the planet"; he uses words expressing extremes: "vast", and strong emotions: "bile, hatred, bigotry". He uses so called "loaded" words: for example, "some ditty" implies a sense of contempt.

* Can you try writing the same ideas in a *non*-emotive way?

Rhetorical questions and exclamations are frequently used in emotive writing, as are vivid similes and metaphors.

FOR PRACTICE

This is the opening of a newspaper article in which a journalist described an interview with disgraced Olympic skater Tonya Harding. Can you pick out the ways in which the writer uses emotive language to capture the reader's interest?

Why Tonya the wicked witch is still running from her past

She answers the door of her rented house like a fugitive, her eyes nervously scanning the empty street. Tonya Harding cannot disguise the fact that she is a young woman on the run from a notorious past.

Her probation may have ended six months ago but she is discovering that, although she recently fled her old neighbourhood in Portland, Oregon, the scent of scandal clings to her like cheap perfume.

Almost four years ago, Harding became the most loathed and vilified sportswoman in the world when she was implicated in the violent plot to cripple Nancy Kerrigan, her American rival for Olympic figure skating glory. It was a crime motivated by monstrous greed and an assault so cowardly that even now, with the next Winter Olympics fast approaching, Americans turn crimson with shame at the mention of her name.

© 'The Mail on Sunday', 9.11.97.

FURTHER PRACTICE

In the following extracts, pick out words and phrases which contribute to the tone. Say what the tone is and explain how the language chosen conveys it. Comment on any features of the language which re-inforce the tone, such as euphemism, oxymoron, hyperbole, unusual juxtapositions, emotive language and so on.

✳   Remember!
     A question on tone is asking you what the writer's choice of words reveals about his *feelings* or his *attitude* to his subject.

1.   Hulk goes into action against the heavies, flinging them about in slow motion. Like Bionic Woman, Six Million Dollar Man and Wonderwoman, Hulk does his action numbers at glacial speed. Emitting slow roars of rage, Hulk runs very slowly towards the enemy, who slowly attempt to make their escape. But no

matter how slowly they run, Hulk runs more slowly. Slowly he picks them up, gradually bangs their heads together, and with a supreme burst of lethargy throws them through the side of a building.

Hardly have the bricks floated to the ground before Hulk is changing back into spindly David Banner, with a sad cello weeping on the soundtrack. One thinks of Frankenstein's monster or the Hunchback of Notre Dame. One thinks of King Kong. One thinks one is being had. Why can't the soft twit cut the soul-searching and just enjoy his ability to swell up and clobber the foe? But David is in quest of "a way to control the raging spirit that dwells within him." Since the series could hardly continue if he finds it, presumably he will be a long time on the trail.

Extract from *The Crystal Bucket* by Clive James

2. Conditions varied from the miserable child-of-all-work, sleeping on a sack under the stairs, in bondage for a few coppers a week and her wretched keep, to the great magnate's house steward, a prosperous member of the middle class.

3. At present the Scottish countryside fulfils a variety of functions. It is a "factory" for the important and basic production industries of farming and forestry. It provides a home for a large population of birds and animals and for the plants and insects that they depend upon. And it serves as a recreational resource for growing numbers of people.

But will the countryside always be able to satisfy all these — and many other — different needs? What about the effects of "progress" in the shape of new motorways, provisions for tourists, industrial demands such as the oil-related developments and so on? How much longer can all the needs continue to be accommodated side by side in the Scottish countryside or are there some things that just cannot go together?

(Comment on the second *paragraph only.)*

4. In this extract, James Herriot, author of the "Vet" books, has found a dog which had been abandoned from a car.

So that was it. He had been dumped. Some time ago the humans he had loved and trusted had opened their car door, hurled him out into an unknown world and driven merrily away. I began to feel sick — physically sick — and a murderous rage flowed through me. Had they laughed, I wondered, these people at the idea of the bewildered little creature toiling vainly behind them?

5. There was a man at Folkstone; I used to meet him on the Lees. He proposed one evening we should go for a long bicycle ride together on the following day and I agreed.

He said: "That's a good-looking machine of yours. How does it run?"
"Oh, like most of them," I answered; "easily enough in the morning; goes a little stiffly after lunch."

He caught hold of it by the front wheel and the fork, and shook it violently.

I said, "Don't do that; you'll hurt it."

I did not see why he should shake it; it had not done anything to him. Besides if it wanted shaking, I was the proper person to shake it. I felt much as I should had he started whacking my dog.

He said, "This front wheel wobbles."

I said, "It doesn't; if you don't wobble it." It didn't wobble, as a matter of fact — nothing worth calling a wobble.

6. In this extract George Orwell, then a policeman in Burma, is being pressured by natives anxious for the sight of blood to kill an elephant which had turned wild.

They had not shown much interest in the elephant when he was merely ravaging their homes, but it was different now that he was going to be shot. It was a bit of fun to them.

Extract from *Shooting an Elephant* by George Orwell

7. Miller leaned forward and began to talk.

"I've listened to you and your twisted mouthings till I'm sick to my guts. What you did sickened and revolted the whole of civilised mankind and left my generation a heritage of shame to live down that's going to take us all the rest of our lives."

8. "It is clearly a reference to the words in a page of some book. Until I am told which page and which book I am powerless."

"Then why has he not indicated the book?"

"Your native shrewdness, my dear Watson, that innate cunning that is the delight of your friends, would surely prevent you from enclosing cipher and message in the same envelope."

9. They were the daughters of a spry, hard-working little washerwoman, who went about from house to house by the day. This was awful enough. But where was Mr Kelvey? Nobody knew for certain. But everybody said he was in prison. So they were the daughters of a washerwoman and a gaolbird. Very nice company for other people's children!

10.

Foreword

To Anthony Pookworthy, Esq., A.B.S., L.L.R.

It is with something more than the natural deference of a tyro at the loveliest, most arduous and perverse of the arts in the presence of a master-craftsman that I lay this book before you. As you know, I have spent some ten years of my creative life in the meaningless and vulgar bustle of newspaper offices. God alone knows what the effect has been on my output of pure literature. I dare not think too much about it — even now.

The life of the journalist is poor, nasty, brutish and short. So is his style. You, who are so adept at the lovely polishing of every grave and lucent phrase, will realise the magnitude of the task which confronted me when I found, after spending ten years as a journalist, learning to say exactly what I meant in short sentences, that I must learn, if I was to achieve Literature and favourable reviews, to write as though I were not quite sure about what I meant but was jolly well going to say something all the same in sentences as long as possible.

It is only because I have in mind all those thousands of persons, not unlike myself, who work in the vulgar and meaningless bustle of offices, shops and homes, and who are not always sure whether a sentence is Literature or whether it is just sheer flapdoodle, that I have adopted the method perfected by the late Herr Baedeker, and firmly marked what I consider the finer passages with one, two or three stars. In such a manner did the good man deal with cathedrals, hotels and paintings by men of genius. There seems no reason why it should not be applied to passages in novels.

It ought to help the reviewers, too.

Extract from *Cold Comfort Farm* by Stella Gibbons

III : IDENTIFYING THE PURPOSE

In the interpretation paper, the last questions will usually ask you to compare and contrast the two passages. You will be invited to compare the two writers' ideas and also the variations in their styles. You will have to apply some of the reading skills described in the first part of this book in order to do this. The following example of this type of question appeared in a recent paper:

Although both writers deal with the morbid topic of the mummy, their styles and tones are different. By looking closely at style and tone, consider the differences and similarities in the two passages.

6 marks

In general, make sure you balance your answer, giving equal weight to both passages. Avoid being vague or woolly — quoting briefly from each passage will avoid this trap. Above all, get the questions done, as they tend to be worth a lot of marks!

Obviously, you will have to demonstrate an understanding of meaning, and also an awareness of sentence structure, diction (word choice) and style. Another relevant area of contrast is to be found in the type of writing it is. Here you must identify the genre, the intended readership and the writer's purpose.

GENRE

The term **Genre**, which basically means "kind of writing", can refer to the three broad groupings in literature, namely prose, poetry and drama. But it can also be used to refer to groups within these groups. In the genre of prose, which is the type of writing used in interpretation tests, we can firstly identify two main sub-genres: fiction and non-fiction, and then find further genres within these. Non-fiction can include academic writing on a subject like medicine or geology and the like. Fiction can include sub-genres such as historical novels, science fiction, detective fiction, children's stories and so on. Occasionally, genres may merge or overlap. Jostein Gaarder's *Sophie's World* is an introduction to philosophy, but it is presented as fiction.

READERSHIP

The passages provided in interpretation tests are of good quality writing aimed at the well-educated general reader. They might, for example, be taken from "broadsheet" or serious newspapers. They do not require any specialised or technical knowledge on the part of the reader. It is helpful for purposes of comparison, however, to have knowledge of the styles of more "down-market" writing, such as is found in "Mills and Boon" romantic fiction or in tabloid newspapers. Some writing is aimed specifically at children or young adults: here you would consider the subject matter and the type of language which would be simpler than usual.

PURPOSE

Writers may have more than one purpose in writing. An academic writer may be aiming simply to instruct, but a travel writer may wish to pass on information and amuse his reader at the same time. A TV or film critic may wish to pass judgement on a film or programme, but also hope to make his readers laugh. Light fiction, such as detective stories, aims merely to entertain readers, but all serious fiction has a moral purpose — to present truths in which the writer believes. Some fiction has a clearly crusading purpose: in *To Kill a Mocking-Bird*, Harper Lee seeks to expose racial injustice, just as a century earlier Dickens had held up to scorn the abuses of the legal profession in *Bleak House*.

TITLES, HEADLINES OR HEADINGS

Headlines or sub-headings of any sort are typical of journalism, and also of factual writing, such as a guide book.

You may be asked to comment on these. The purpose of any heading is to attract the reader's attention and tempt him to read on; it may also summarise the passage briefly.

* Bold type : catches the reader's eye and attracts his attention.

* Questions arouse a reader's curiosity. He will read on to find out if the question is answered.

* Short sentences are understood at a glance.

* Alliteration, rhyme and jingles have impact.

* Puns or mystifying headlines amuse and intrigue the reader and entice him to read on.

Applying the skills

Read the following passage. It is followed by a commentary discussing features of style and tone and identifying the genre:

> "Medina," I yelled, "I've a rope. I'm going to send it down to you. Get your arm in the loop."
>
> My loop was a large one and I think he had got both arms through it. He was a monstrous weight, limp and dead as a sack. Inch by inch I was drawing him in, till I realised the danger. The rope was grating on the sharp brink beyond the chimney and might at any moment be cut by a knife-edge.
>
> "Medina" — my voice must have been like a wild animal's scream — "this is too dangerous. I'm going to let you down a bit so that you can traverse. Try and climb back into the chimney."
>
> He found some sort of foothold, and for a moment there was a relaxation of the strain.
>
> "Cheer up," I cried. "Once in the chimney you're safe. Sing out when you reach it."
>
> The answer out of the darkness was a sob. I think giddiness must have overtaken him, or that atrophy of muscle which is the peril of rock-climbing.

Continued on next page

Suddenly the rope scorched my fingers and a shock came which dragged me to the very edge of the abyss. I still believe that I could have saved him if I had had the use of both my hands, for I could have guided the rope away from that fatal knife-edge. I knew it was hopeless, but I put every ounce of strength and will into the effort to swing it with its burden into the chimney. He gave me no help, for I think — I hope — that he was unconscious. Next second the strands had parted, and I fell back with a sound in my ears which I pray God I may never hear again — the sound of a body rebounding dully from crag to crag, and then a long soft rumbling of screes like a snowslip.

The extract is adapted from the final few paragraphs of *The Three Hostages* by John Buchan, a thriller first published in 1924.

Commentary: This passage is written in the first person and is narrative in style. It appears to be part of a novel as there are characters involved such as "Medina" and direct speech is used. It appears to be an all-action thriller, as it describes a dramatic struggle on a cliff-top resulting in the death of one character. The language is melodramatic: "the very edge of the abyss". Such a book would be intended for the entertainment of fans of this genre. The language is slightly archaic : "Sing out"; "a monstrous weight", suggesting the book may be at least fifty years old.

Of special note is the skilful building up of suspense, with the tense dialogue, and the structure of the last sentence. The sentence is prolonged after the dash with several phrases and there is also a good onomatopoeic effect to put over the idea of a body falling down a cliff face.

FOR PRACTICE

Each of the following pieces of writing belongs to a particular genre. In pairs or small groups, read and discuss each extract, and then write a short report. Pick out ideas and language features which help you to identify *(a)* the genre and *(b)* the intended readership. Then *(c)* mention any additional features of the writing which seem in any way special.

1. Up to about twenty years ago, it was thought that protons and neutrons were "elementary" particles, but experiments in which protons were collided with other protons or electrons at high speeds indicated that they were in fact made up of smaller particles. These particles were named quarks by the Caltech physicist Murray Gell-Mann, who won the Nobel prize in 1969 for his work on them. The origin of the name is an enigmatic quotation from James Joyce: "Three quarks for Muster Mark!" The word *quark* is supposed to be pronounced like *quart*, but with a *k* at the end instead of a *t*, but is usually pronounced to rhyme with *lark*. There are a number of different varieties of quarks; there are thought to be at least six "flavours", which we call up, down, strange, charmed, bottom and top. A proton contains two up quarks, and one down quark; a neutron contains two down and one up. We can create particles made up of the other quarks, but these all have a much greater mass and decay very rapidly into protons and neutrons.

2. *Tip tap, tip tap, tip tap tip!*

   "Now what can that be?" said the Tailor of Gloucester, jumping up from his chair. The dresser was covered with crockery and pipkins, willow pattern plates, and teacups and mugs.

   The tailor crossed the kitchen, and stood quite still beside the dresser, listening and peering through his spectacles. Again from under a tea-cup, came those funny little noises —

   Tip tap, tip tap, tip tap tip!

   "This is very peculiar," said the Tailor of Gloucester; and he lifted up the tea-cup which was upside down.

   Out stepped a little live lady mouse, and made a curtsey to the tailor! Then she hopped away down off the dresser, and under the wainscot.

3. It was the day my grandmother exploded. I sat in the crematorium, listening to my Uncle Hamish quietly snoring in harmony to Bach's Mass in B Minor, and I reflected that it always seemed to be death that drew me back to Gallanach.

I looked at my father, sitting two rows away in the front line of seats in the cold, echoing chapel. His broad, greying-brown head was massive above his tweed jacket (a black arm-band was his concession to the solemnity of the occasion). His ears were moving in a slow, oscillatory manner, rather in the way John Wayne's shoulders moved when he walked; my father was grinding his teeth.

Probably he was annoyed that my grandmother had chosen religious music for her funeral ceremony. I didn't think she had done it to upset him; doubtless she had simply liked the tune, and had not anticipated the effect its non-secular nature might have on her eldest son.

My younger brother, James, sat to my father's left. It was the first time in years I'd seen him without his Walkman, and he looked distinctly uncomfortable, fiddling with his single earring. To my father's right my mother sat, upright and trim, neatly filling a black coat and sporting a dramatic black hat shaped like a flying saucer. The UFO dipped briefly to one side as she whispered something to my father.

4. But my grandmother's greatest assets were her bound feet, called in Chinese "three-inch golden lilies" (san-tsun-gin-lian.) This meant she walked "like a tender young willow shoot in a spring breeze," as Chinese connoisseurs of women traditionally put it.

My grandmother's feet had been bound when she was two years old. Her mother, who herself had bound feet, first wound a piece of white cloth about twenty feet long round her feet, bending all the toes except the big toe inward and under the sole. Then she placed a large stone on top to crush the arch. My grandmother screamed in agony and begged her to stop. Her mother had to stick a cloth into her mouth to gag her.

The process lasted several years. Even after the bones had been broken, the feet had to be bound day and night in thick cloth because the moment they were released they would try to recover. For years my grandmother lived in relentless, excruciating pain. When she pleaded with her mother to untie the bindings, her mother would weep and tell her that unbound feet would ruin her entire life, and that she was doing it for her own future happiness.

5.   Down by the sea there was something strange and wonderful. It was a horse 100 metres high, with a mane and tail of blue and scarlet feathers. Priam examined it keenly.

"We'll place the horse in the city square, then everyone will remember the day the cowardly Greeks sailed home."

Through the town it rolled, its head level with the roof-tops of the highest houses, until it came to a halt in the city square in front of the church of the Goddess. Then Priam ordered, "Let the celebrations begin!"

There were fireworks, street parties, hundreds of bands, free food and free booze. The Trojans hadn't partied like this since the war had begun. By three o'clock in the morning, everyone had crawled exhausted to their beds except for a few drunken revellers who'd passed out in the city square.

The horse stood still and silent. Nothing stirred.

Then there were footsteps. It was Helen with her new Trojan boyfriend. He had permed blond hair, chunky jewellery and his shirt was unbuttoned to the waist.

Helen patted the horse's leg. "Suppose this is all a trick," she whispered. "Suppose the horse is full of Greek soldiers."

"Oh, come on," laughed the boyfriend. "Don't be ridiculous."

6.   Colossal self-confidence is perhaps the hallmark of the aristocrat. He goes through life unafraid; he doesn't question his motives or feel guilty about his actions. When I went shooting in Northumberland last summer I noticed a beautiful blond young man in a red sweater at the next butt. Why didn't he have to wear green camouflage like the rest of us, I asked.

"Because he's a duke's son," said my host. "He can do what he likes."

Not answerable to other people, the aristocrat is often unimaginative, spoilt, easily irritated and doesn't flinch from showing it. If he wants to eat his peas with his knife he does so.

"Dear Kate," said Henry V, "You and I cannot be confined within the weak list of a country's fashion; we are the makers of manners, Kate; and the liberty that follows out places stops the mouth of all find-faults."

As the makers of manners, many of the aristocracy, while feeling they have a duty towards the community, are indifferent to public opinion.

Not caring a stuff what people think also leads to a rich vein of eccentricity: the Marquess of Londonderry throwing soup at a fly that was irritating him in a restaurant, and Sir Antony Eden's father hurling a barometer out of the window into the pouring rain, yelling, "See for yourself, you bloody thing." Or there was the imperious peer who, when he missed a train, ordered the station-master to get him another one.

7. To withdraw her thoughts, however, from the subject of her misfortunes, she attempted to read, but her attention wandered from the page, and, at length, she threw aside the book, and determined to explore the adjoining chambers of the castle. Her imagination was pleased with the view of ancient grandeur, and an emotion of melancholy awe awakened all its powers, as she walked through rooms, obscure and desolate, where no footsteps had passed probably for many years, and remembered the strange history of the former possessor of the edifice. This brought to her recollection the veiled picture, which had attracted her curiosity on the preceding night, and she resolved to examine it. As she passed through the chambers that led to this, she found herself somewhat agitated; its connection with the late lady of the castle and the conversation of Annette, together with the circumstance of the veil, throwing a mystery over the subject, that excited a faint degree of terror. But a terror of this nature, as it occupies and expands the mind, and elevates it to high expectation, is purely sublime, and leads us, by a kind of fascination, to seek even the object, from which we appear to shrink.

Emily passed on with faltering steps, and having paused a moment at the door, before she attempted to open it, she then hastily entered the chamber, and went towards the picture, which appeared to be enclosed in a frame of uncommon size, that hung in a dark part of the room. She paused again, and then, with a timid hand, lifted the veil; but instantly let it fall — perceiving that what it concealed was no picture, and, before she could leave the chamber, she dropped senseless on the floor.

8. I saw the bright flags of Butlin's Minehead and vowed to make a visit. With its barracks-like buildings and its forbidding fences it had the prison look of the Butlin's at Bognor. A prison look was also an army camp look, and just as depressing. This one was the more scary for being brightly painted. It had been tacked together out of plywood and tin panels in primary colours. I had not seen flimsier buildings in England. They were so ugly they were not pictured anywhere in the Butlin's brochure, but instead shown as simplified floor plans in blue diagrams. One of Butlin's boasts was: "No dirty dishes to wash!" Another was: "There is absolutely no need to queue!" No dish-washing, no queuing — it came near to parody, like a vacation in a Polish joke.

9. The Cyrastorian pushed his long fingers against his temples. He could feel himself steadily moving from the centre of The Will, out into the peripheral zones of its influence. Sometimes Gezra, The Elder, felt that he had been wrong to pursue this line of work beyond his allotted span. It was as if he could feel the very chill of deep space, insinuating itself into his flesh and bone, through the translucent aura of The Will, which protected him and all his world's sons and daughters.

In the darkness of his craft, illuminated only by the screen which panned up images of the observed planet, The Appropriate Behaviour Compliance Elder for this sector pondered as to the likely destiny of the rogue youth's ship. Earth seemed almost too obvious. After all, their specimen had been from that world. Specimen, Gezra smiled across his thin lips, he would have to stop using such a pejorative, demeaning term. After all, the Earthman had been inducted, electing to stay a part of Cyrastorian culture, rather than return home with a memory wipe, and all in return for strangely modest rewards. There was little to be gained in attempting to understand the primitive psyche of the Earth creature.

10. In *Owner Occupied*, apparently the pilot show for a new sit-com, Robert Hardy was given another chance to employ the Cherman accent he brought to such perfection when playing Prince Albert in *Edward VII*. This time he was a Cherman officer occupying one of the Channel Islands (I think it must have been Chersey) during World War II. Hannah Gordon was the cuddlesome local beauty who despised everything he stood for. But Hardy was such a luffable Cherman officer that she plainly found it difficult to resist his charm. That must have been how he got his Iron Cross and wound stripe — charming the Poles to death.

Hannah's father ran the hotel which the Cherman officer had requisitioned as his headquarters. The former was a kind of *Hotel Sahara* with less sand and more . . . well, crap, actually. There was a good deal of unchentlemanly behaviour from some of the locals during the Cherman occupation of the Channel Islands. If we see some of that, the series might chust work. Otherwise it will be a load of chunk.

11.   The wire entanglements are torn to pieces. Yet they offer some obstacle. We see the storm-troops coming. Our artillery opens fire. Machine-guns rattle, rifles crack. The charge works its way across.

We recognise the smooth distorted faces, the helmets: they are French. They have already suffered heavily when they reach the remnants of the barbed wire entanglements. A whole line has gone down before our machine-guns; then we have a lot of stoppages and they come nearer.

I see one of them, his face upturned, fall into a wire cradle. His body collapses, his hands remain suspended as though he were praying. Then his body drops clean away and only his hands with the stumps of his arms, shot off, now hang in the wire.

12.   **TEMPLETON'S CARPET FACTORY**, off Glasgow Green.

You're not seeing things! This ornate Victorian factory really is modelled on the Doge's Palace in Venice. The reason? Well, when the famous carpet manufacturers, James Templeton and Co., proposed a factory on the site in the 1880s, the City Fathers decided that as it was so near to the much-treasured Glasgow Green (*see page 111*), it had to be a truly beautiful building. Templeton nominated William Leiper as the architect and Leiper chose one of his favourite buildings, the Doge's Palace, as his theme. Elaborately decorated with coloured, glazed brick, battlements, arches and pointed windows it is a most intriguing sight so near to the city centre. The factory, which produced carpets for royal weddings and christenings and covered many a famous floor, closed in 1979 and the building is now used as offices for small businesses.

Open: viewing from outside only, all the time.

EXTRA . . . EXTRA . . . The brickwork of the building is of such high quality that apprentice bricklayers often come here to study and learn from it.

13.   Wayland crossed the outward and inward castle yard, and the great arched passage, which led to the bottom of the little winding stair that gave access to the chambers of Mervyn's Tower.

He congratulated himself on having escaped the various perils of his journey, and was in the act of ascending by two steps at once, when he observed that the shadow of a man, thrown from a door which stood ajar, darkened the opposite wall of the staircase. He ascended as high as the suspicious spot — he ascended a few yards farther — the door was still ajar, and he was doubtful whether to advance or retreat, when it was suddenly thrown wide open.

"Who the devil art thou? And what seek'st thou in this part of the castle? March into that chamber, and be hanged to thee!"

"I am no dog to go at every man's whistle," said Wayland, affecting a confidence which was belied by a timid shake in his voice.

"Sayst thou me so? — Come hither. If thou be'st so fond of this tower, my friend, thou shalt see its foundations, good twelve feet below the bed of the lake, and tenanted by certain jolly toads, snakes, and so forth, which thou wilt find mighty good company. Therefore, once more I ask you in fair play, who thou art, and what thou seek'st here?"

YOU WILL FIND THE ACTUAL SOURCES OF THE EXTRACTS IN
APPENDIX II. (Pages 110-111.)

PART TWO

Writing in Focus

WRITING IN FOCUS (1)

SHARON THE SHARK

This is a skilfully written piece of journalism in which the writer contrasts how sharks are depicted in films with what they are *really* like.

   ✳   it combines **humour** with more serious **discussion**
   ✳   it develops a line of **argument** in a series of **paragraphs**
   ✳   it has an effective **conclusion**

Read the article carefully. The detailed analysis of it which follows will show you how the writer manages to achieve his effects. Remember that when a particular literary term is printed in heavy type (such as **alliteration**) you will find a detailed explanation of it in Part One of this book.

SHARON THE SHARK

Humans are more of a threat to sharks than they are to humans

In 1975 *Jaws* set the hearts of its audiences thumping to its theme tune. A piscine serial killer had been born — and with it a host of ever more improbable sequences. Box offices enjoyed a feeding-frenzy, while the man-eating monster finned through its films, hoovering up holidaymakers as it went.

Now research from the University of California suggests that the film-makers' facts are as false as their rubber fishes. Scientific experiments show that the great white shark is a fastidious eater. The peckish predator finds human snacks about as appetising as stale Ryvita. It prefers the fat-rich flesh of seals to bathing beach babes.

While we enjoy a mammalian complicity with the dolphin or whale, the shark is ostracised and misunderstood. The great white is one of the most mysterious creatures in the ocean. Survivor of more than 400 million years of evolution, it has eluded — or utterly ignored — human efforts to understand it. Imprisoned in an aquarium, it almost immediately dies. Some suspect that it may be one of the few creatures which we can never know. Yet, at the apex of the ocean food chain, it plays a vital role. Biologists suspect that the entire marine ecosystem would be unbalanced by its loss.

Big game fishers have pursued the great white towards the margins of extinction. Fortunately it has now been listed as an endangered species in South Africa and Australia. We have become more of a threat to this species than it is to us. Far more sharks are killed daily to supply fin soup to Chinese restaurants than people are attacked in a year.

Of course there are areas where surfers and divers run a real risk. A species such as the great white is known to "mouth" its prey before eating it: to catch it between its jaws to test it for palatability. Its serrated teeth are so sharp that even this is enough to sever tendons and bone. But technology is tackling this. The Protective Oceanic Device has recently been pioneered. It safeguards swimmers by encircling them with an electric field that even potentially lethal sharks appear unwilling to enter. Similar technology is being developed to fence off bathing beaches.

In the 19th century, Herman Melville saw the whale as a lethal leviathan. Now it is a Hollywood hero. Last year, children all over the world were sobbing at the plight of the poor imprisoned Willie. Now it is time for Sharon the Shark to take her starring role.

Sharon the Shark from 'The Times', London, 18.7.97.

❋ *How does the writer combine humour with serious discussion?*

Look again at paragraphs one and two. You will immediately notice the use of **alliteration**. List all the examples of this that you can find in the first two paragraphs.

You will probably have found five or six — and you may feel that is rather too many in the course of fifteen lines.

> FOR DISCUSSION
> Is this a case of a writer trying too hard to be "stylish" or is he doing this on purpose in order to achieve a particular effect? If so, what effect is he aiming at? Is there any connection between the style of writing here and the type of film being discussed?

The opening paragraphs also employ **imagery** which adds to the humorous effect because it often depends on **exaggeration**. In the four examples which follow, try to identify *(a)* whether the writer is using a particular type of imagery (e.g. a **metaphor**) and *(b)* how exactly the comparison succeeds in creating humour.

> *A piscine serial killer*
> *Box offices enjoyed a feeding frenzy*
> *The film-makers' facts are as false as their rubber fishes*
> *The peckish predator finds human snacks about as appetising as stale Ryvita.*

Now read paragraph three again. In what ways is the **tone** of this different from the previous two?

Choose a word from the list that follows which you think would describe the tone *(a)* of paragraphs one and two and *(b)* of paragraph three.

thoughtful	flippant	sarcastic	light-hearted
melodramatic	analytical	objective	reflective

Write down three words or phrases from the third paragraph that seem to you to be particularly different in tone from the previous two.

✳ *How does the writer develop an argument in a series of paragraphs?*

A writer might have plenty of very convincing points to make, but they will have much greater impact on the reader if they are presented in the right order, so that one point leads up to the next and everything builds up to a strong conclusion.

Paragraphs 3, 4 and 5 of *Sharon the Shark* each deal with a separate aspect of the topic.

Summarise the main point made in each paragraph, using only one sentence for each.

You will probably have found that the first sentence of each paragraph was the most helpful in signposting the direction of the argument. Try to explain how each of the following points is developed in the rest of the paragraph.

Paragraph 3: *The shark is ostracised and misunderstood.*

Paragraph 4: *The great white shark is now at "the margins of extinction".*

Paragraph 5: *Surfers and divers run a real risk.*

At what point in paragraph 5 could the writer perhaps have started a new paragraph? Justify your choice.

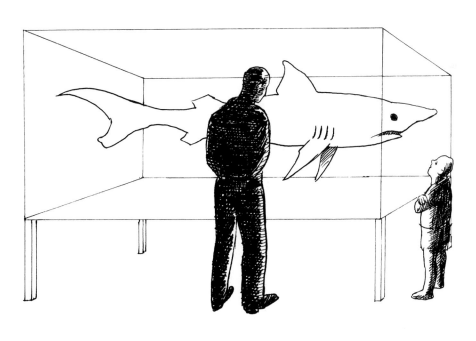

Think of two ways in which the last four lines remind you of the opening two paragraphs.

The last sentence sums up the whole point that the writer wants to make. Explain what his point actually is.

Compare what you have just written with the author's last sentence. Which would have more impact on the reader? Why?

WRITING IN FOCUS (2)

THE SPOILS OF CHILDHOOD

Journalist Libby Purves begins this article with a description of a new department store aimed at children, and moves on to a more general reflection on how society's attitudes to children have changed in the course of the writer's lifetime.

Read the passage right through. Then re-read it more slowly in conjunction with the comments and questions on the left-hand side which will help you to think about the stylistic techniques used by the writer. Technical terms are printed in heavy type and explanations of these can be found in part one of this book.

The writer spends some time elaborating her description of the interior of the store.

Why are these particular details included?

Boom and consume, shop till you flop: Chelsea has a new department store. It is upmarket, beautifully fitted with wide, comfortable galleries and a stage-designer's vision. There is an indoor clock tower and beautiful barley-sugar twist banisters on the wide Edwardian staircases; a soda fountain, hair salon, clothes and shoes, and books and furniture, and bikes and games. No, not for you: everything on sale is for children under ten.

Why are so many "ands" used here?

*The purpose of this build-up is to make the last sentence have more impact as it is unexpected. This technique is known as **anti-climax**.*
What is the tone of the first sentence of this paragraph?
The writer imagines what the reader's response might be. What social stereotypes is she drawing on here?

Ah well, you say — *Chelsea. *The King's Road. Drifting *Sloane mums trying to fill Nanny's day off; affluent access-daddies desperate for something to do which doesn't involve the swimming-pool

* Chelsea, King's Road and Sloane Square are fashionable parts of London.

changing room. But it is not just Chelsea: there is another one twice the size opening soon in Manchester, and plans for the rest of the nation. And for Europe.

These two paragraphs contain straight-forward reporting. What differences in the style do you notice compared to the previous two?

*Comment on the **word choice** of "self-deprecating maverick", using your dictionary for assistance if necessary.*

Children's department stores are the latest brainwave from Tim Waterstone, the gentle, self-deprecating maverick who changed the face of British bookselling in the eighties. He has called the stores Daisy & Tom after his three-year-old daughter and the son of one of his backers. But his personal credentials for starting such an enterprise are impeccable.

"Look, I have eight children, from 34 down to three," he says. "I want to create a shop which pays children the compliment of offering good quality in surroundings designed for them. We will not be selling tat. Lots of good quality wooden toys."

*Now Libby Purves returns to anticipating possible readers' reactions, using the technique of **rhetorical question**.*

Her own response is to praise one particular aspect of the store owner's philosophy. Explain what it is. (Clue: look up the word "quixotically" in your dictionary).

Decadent? Institutionalised spoiling? Western sentimental fantasy, insulting to a world where six-year-olds toil in dark factories? Perhaps. But it is very pretty, and it would be hard to begrudge Mr. Waterstone another success. At least his commercial policy is quixotically fixed on pretty shops and friendly atmosphere; unlike that of bigger, colder-eyed public companies who entice children into an atmosphere of hard-sell.

The conjunction "but" turns the discussion away from an examination of one particular shop towards a wider theme. What contrast between the activities of today's children and those of a previous generation is suggested?

But the advent of Daisy & Tom does make you reflect on what has happened to Britain over the past few decades. It is not so long since we were a nation which dressed its young in cutdown adult clothing. Children were expected to watch their dads play

WRITING IN FOCUS

*This paragraph uses the technique of **listing** examples. The general point is not explicitly stated but can be deduced from the examples given. Why are these particular examples chosen and what point is being made?*

*Comment on the **tone** of this sentence. (Look back at pages 47–50 for help.)*

Again, instead of stating that there are still youngsters who are unaware of what is considered "sophisticated", the writer gives examples of their activities.

*Explain the function of the **colon** in this sentence.*

How does this short sentence act as a turning point in the argument?

In your own words, explain why adults want to buy gifts and treats for children, basing your answer on the last two paragraphs.

cricket on Saturday, and to wriggle on chairs during long, boring Sunday visits to great-granny with no reward but a dry macaroon. No McDonald's, no inflatable ball-ponds and foam-rubber Wonderworlds. No Nike Airs or Docs for us. Young reader, you may not believe this, but in the dark 1960s it was commonplace for girls to *wear their school shoes in the holidays.*

Of course, there are still children who go biking on their own, build dens in the hedge and roll in mud; who still think it is a big deal to go into Ipswich, and have not discovered that C&A is not a designer label. But television soon shows them the new kiddy consumer deal, and eventually they want it. There is no point parents inveighing against commercial exploitation of childhood: we encourage it. The advertisers' theory of "pester power" and direct advertising to children would not work if we didn't give in.

But we do. It is easy to become addicted to the moment when a loved child widens his eyes and gasps with amazement at the miraculous gift or treat the power of our money has brought. The marketeers are only giving us what they reckon we will buy. Not just novelty or cuteness, but a whole package designed to reassure us — for money — that the world welcomes our children and cares what happens to them. The childless complain that "every damn thing is geared to kids." But they are wrong. What has really happened is that we see daily how dangerous, how uncertain, how bad and sad things are for the world's children; and it makes us want to get out the plastic card and buy our own fairyland.

*"Gild the cage" is an example of a **metaphor**. What is being compared to what? Think about the implications of this comparison.*

So we keep the children indoors and gild the cage with bedroom televisions and computer consoles. We fear that they won't get jobs, will be poisoned by pollution or burnt by the hole in the ozone layer. If you live without faith or much hope, it makes sense to fulfil children's dreams right now, while they are small and the dreams are simple.

Extract from *The Spoils of Childhood* © Libby Purves, 1997.

✳   Now that you have studied this passage in depth, look back at the title, which contains a **pun**. Can you explain the two ways in which this title could be understood?

✳   Does Libby Purves take an **objective** or a **subjective** approach to her subject? Select three pieces of evidence to back up your view.

WRITING IN FOCUS (3)

THE DANGLING MAN

In this article, the poet and author Will Self is reviewing *Storms of Silence*, a book by mountaineer Joe Simpson. He begins by discussing an earlier book by the same author, *Touching the Void*, which he had very much enjoyed, and then he goes on to explain why he is disappointed by the new book.

*What do you notice about the **structure** of the first three sentences? How effective is it as the opening of a review of a mountaineering book?*

I like reading books about mountaineering. I like reading books about mountaineering while lying down. I like reading books about mountaineering while lying down in low-lying country.

*The word "schadenfreude" means enjoying someone else's misfortune. How might the **context** have told you this?*

The more vertiginous and alarming the position of the climber, the better pleased I am. Ideally, I'd like a mountaineering book set entirely on a near-vertical ice face, told (in real time) from the point of view of a climber in imminent danger of falling some thousands of metres to certain death. Juxtaposing this with my own earthbound condition would give me a thrill of the most profound *schadenfreude*.

*Can you show how the first sentence in this paragraph acts as a **link**?*

From this almost subterranean perspective, the first book by Joe Simpson that I read, *Touching the Void*, was a minor classic, the tale of his rapid, two-man ascent of the West Face of Siula Grande, a particularly nasty little 6,000 metre peak in the Peruvian Andes. Following the ascent — tautly described and dangerous in the extreme — came the descent. Unfortunately for Simpson this was somewhat swifter than planned, since he fell 300 feet of it in two separate accidents. In the first he broke his leg. His climbing partner, Simon Yates, heroically belayed him down 2,500 feet of sheer ice face, before he ran out of rope and had to cut the injured man loose or face certain death himself.

*In paragraph 3, the reviewer compares this book with an earlier one by the same author. He combines a slightly **tongue-in-cheek tone** with a more **serious** one in which he expresses genuine admiration. Can you pick out a phrase which is an example of each? (Make clear which is which.)*

Simpson fell into a deep crevasse, but survived. It took him six hellish days to get out and crawl back down the mountain to the base camp. He was only just in time to catch his companions before they departed. *Touching the Void* maintained the tensility and narrative glissade of a frozen rope throughout. Judging by the slack feel of *Storms of Silence*, its successor, this must have been in part because Simpson confined himself to the technicalities of getting up mountains — and the brutalities of falling off them.

*Comment on the **metaphor** in the last two sentences of this paragraph. Why is it particularly suitable to use for a book on this topic?*

It was no surprise to find, in the new book, that having been told he had no chance of recovering well enough to climb again, he fought his way back upright, and then back up. Certain kinds of physical courage must be predicated on a determined lack of imagination. Of course, it is evident that the question of the will-to-risk embodied in mountaineering still has a compelling hold on the popular unconscious. Simpson supplies the antithesis, the dark side. What he's really good at isn't climbing mountains — it's falling off them.

In what way do you think lack of imagination might contribute to an impression of courage?

Can you write down in your own words the aspect of mountaineering that the author says has "such a compelling hold" on our imaginations. Do you agree with him?

Storms of Silence is bound to disappoint on this score, consisting as it does largely of attempts by Simpson to get up high enough for a really spectacular fall, and of his being frustrated by old injuries, failure to acclimatise to high altitude and other more numinous impediments. As Simpson gave up on peak after peak, the little angel on my right shoulder applauded, while the little devil on my left cursed, cheated yet again of that delicious thrill which would only come when he was well and truly a dangling man.

*What is the **tone** of the first sentence of this paragraph?*

Can you explain the reviewer's contrasting thoughts towards the risks Simpson takes which he personifies as "the little angel on my right shoulder" and "the little devil on my left"?

WRITING IN FOCUS

Continued on next page

*Comment on the **choice of words** used in Simpson's title,* Storms of Silence.

Why does the reviewer object to Simpson choosing the phrase Storms of Silence *as the title for his book?*

One other quibble concerns the book's title. In a book called *Storms of Silence*, one might have hoped for some. Simpson reminds us throughout that he climbs while mainlining sound through a Walkman. That's pretty gauche for those of us armchair mountaineers who want our impressions of the sea of clouds minus a soundtrack. But when I learned what sort of noise he had been listening to — *White Wedding* by Billy Idol; Sibelius I could have borne — my patience snapped. Much as I admire him, I think Simpson really should stick to what he does best — falling.

✳ Can you identify at least two purposes the writer had in writing this review? Give evidence for these. Rank them in order of importance, giving your reasons.

✳ The writer has used a very personal and humorous style for his review, rather than a straighter, more serious one. Consider why a more serious approach might be preferred by some readers. Which style would appeal to you more, and why?

WRITING IN FOCUS (4)

IDOL THOUGHTS

In this article, first published in *The Scotsman*, Laurie Maguire was reviewing one of the many biographies written about the film actress, Marilyn Monroe. In this part of the article, the author is considering why Monroe's "legend" is so enduring.

*Do you know the **literal** meaning of the word reincarnated? Use a dictionary to find it if necessary. In what way can Marilyn Monroe be said to have been "reincarnated" after her death?*

Since Marilyn Monroe's death she has reached cult status of almost mythic proportions. She has been reincarnated not only in "illustrated biographies" but on posters and magazine covers, T-shirts and wallpaper. Some shops which specialise in wrapping paper and postcards have whole sections devoted to Marilyn and that other long-lasting film star who also died young, James Dean. Each year in New York there is the Marilyn Monroe Memorabilia Show and Sale. As other stars come and go, Monroe's popularity seems constant. She is still able to bewitch fans many of whom were not even born when her films were first released. What, after all these years, makes Monroe so enduring?

What two aspects of Monroe's character does this quotation illustrate?

*How does the **context** help you explain the word "epitomised"?*

When asked what she thought of being the world's number one sex symbol, Marilyn was reported to have answered: "I never understood it. I always thought symbols were things you clash together." It was a typical remark from the star who epitomised the dumb blonde. Yet, Marilyn Monroe was far more than a symbol of sex. She was a symbol of her times — the fifties that brought forth the H-Bomb, rock 'n' roll and the fish-finned Chevrolet.

The "American Dream" is the belief that, in the United States, anyone can become rich and successful, no matter who they are or where they come from. Was Marilyn Monroe living proof of this?

Along with the Stars and Stripes and the New York skyline, Monroe embodies America and the American Dream. She is also a symbol of womanhood once appropriated as the patron saint of the women's movement. Exploited and abused by men, she yearned to be taken seriously.

Small wonder, then, that over the years she has become all things to all men — and women. And if imitation is the sincerest form of flattery then Marilyn can lay claim to some flattering duplicates. In her own lifetime Jayne Mansfield and Diana Dors battled for a share of Monroe's magic. Since her death stars like Goldie Hawn and Madonna have owed much to Monroe. No one has ever come close to the original, however, and no other female star before or since has ever been held in quite the same reverence as the tragic sex goddess Marilyn Monroe.

In the last sentence of this paragraph Marilyn Monroe is referred to as a "goddess". Can you find two words in the first paragraph which also show her being regarded in this way? Can you explain your choice?

Her iconic status goes far beyond her roles in such films as *The Seven Year Itch* and *Some Like It Hot*. She is as famous for simply being the much-photographed Marilyn Monroe. At one time she was the most photographed woman in the world. Her love affair with the lens was legendary. The actress Constance Collier neatly summed up Monroe's unique presence: "It's so fragile and subtle it can only be caught by the camera; like a hummingbird in flight only the camera can capture the poetry of it."

Using a dictionary if necessary, explain the phrase "iconic status".

*Constance Collier uses a "humming-bird" **image** to describe the actress. What special qualities of Marilyn do you think this captures?*

Part of Monroe's mystique is the vulnerability she had about her. Marilyn, or Norma-Jean as she was born, has been called the classic case of the neglected and abused child. Her father deserted her and her mother lived on the edge of nervous collapse and was later institutionalised.

*Show how the first sentence in this paragraph has a **linking** function.*

The story of Monroe's tragi-glamorous life makes her the ideal idol for any mixed-up adolescent. She has become the guardian angel of millions of bed-sits. Her benign influence looking down from four-colour posters says: "Look, I had a lousy childhood, too. My parents were never there when I needed them. I know what loneliness is, but look! I made it. I became a star. So pull yourself together, honey!"

In your own words, explain why the author believes Monroe appeals particularly to "mixed-up adolescents."

Monroe appeals to everyone's insecurity. In many

photographs an unmistakable sadness flickers in the eyes. It is a haunting and painfully endearing quality no other film star has ever possessed.

How, according to the author, has Monroe's early death contributed to her continuing popularity?

What do you understand by "teenage angst"? Use a dictionary if necessary.

Monroe's premature death, like her vulnerability, is an important key to her durability. If that other icon of teenage angst, James Dean, was too fast to live, then Marilyn was too sweet. Marilyn's early demise makes her story more haunting in that it has not been allowed to play itself to its logical conclusion.

In this paragraph the author makes a comparison with the Queen. What is gained by it, do you think?

How effective do you find the imagery in this paragraph?

But perhaps most importantly of all Marilyn is caught in aspic. If she were alive today she would be the same age as the Queen. Her death has suspended her forever like a beautiful butterfly in a glass case. She is frozen forever.

Courtesy of *The Scotsman*

W
R
I
T
I
N
G

I
N

F
O
C
U
S

✳   In your own words, give two pieces of evidence which show women admired Monroe as well as men. Explain the reasons for this.

✳   Which piece of evidence mentioned in the article do you feel provides the most convincing proof of Monroe's continuing appeal? Explain why.

✳   The author uses a **pun** in the title of this article. Can you explain the two meanings? How appropriate do you find the pun?

PART THREE

Interpretation Practice

SCOTTISH WOMAN

THE STATUS OF WOMEN

In the following passage, Maggie Craig argues that the place of women in Scottish history has been neglected or distorted.

PASSAGE 1

We might all be Jock Tamson's bairns, but from the reading of much Scottish history you'd never guess that Jock and his wife had daughters as well as sons. Even modern writers —who should, one would think, know better — manage to convey the impression that generations of Scotsmen produced further generations of the
5 same without recourse to the female sex at all.

The romanticisers do give us the standard heroines: Mary Queen of Scots, Jenny Geddes and, of course, Flora MacDonald. There she stands in front of Inverness Castle, her faithful dog by her side, shading her eyes as she looks in the direction of Skye.

10 She's also conveniently silent, like most women in Scottish history, gagged not so much by the restrictions of their own times as by the wilful blindness of subsequent historians.

Other than icons like Flora, Scotswomen appear in histories in strictly delineated areas: women in the labour force, sexuality, witchcraft — a sort of
15 bolt-on accessory to male history. Even the significant works which have appeared in recent years, some of which even have a special chapter devoted to women, tend to ghettoise them in these same spheres of activity.

Sorry, lassies, say the historians, but you've got to face facts — that's where you were — in menial jobs, contributing to the illegitimacy rate in Ayrshire or
20 Aberdeen — we've got a nice graph on that one — or being burned at the stake in front of Edinburgh Castle. The rest of you were at home stirring the porridge. Not much to write about there.

Continued on next page

This is just not the full picture. The smallest amount of digging will turn up many Scotswomen over the centuries involved in many different areas of life.
25 We can go right back to Pictish society, run on a matriarchal system of descent. We can look at women like Isobel, Countess of Fife, who set the crown on Robert the Bruce's head and suffered dearly as a result. What about the female Covenanting martyrs whose stories still need to be investigated?

What about Anne Leith who went out to Culloden with two other women on
30 the afternoon of the battle to do what they could for the wounded and the dying and who stayed in Inverness afterwards, badgering the authorities to give the Jacobite prisoners better treatment? What about Anne McKay, who helped a young officer escape from Inverness and who suffered physical maltreatment as a result, her teenage son being beaten to death by the redcoats
35 in reprisal?

Why has no-one erected a statue to these women or the many others like them? Why do we not see their pictures on shortbread tin lids? The information which tells their stories is there — in original documents in libraries and archives throughout the country.

40 Our history matters. Only a country which knows where it has been can work out where it is going. The historian, constantly aware of his or her own prejudices and cultural conditioning, should strive to see the whole picture, from as many points of view as possible. We have moved a long way from the belief that history is about only the great and the powerful. Women's history
45 is part of people's history too — the story of all the bairns of Adam. And, of course, Eve, too.

Courtesy of *The Herald*

The following passage is an abridged version of part of a speech delivered by Hillary Clinton to the United Nations Fourth World Conference on Women in Beijing, China, September 1995.

PASSAGE 2

This conference is truly a celebration — a celebration of the contributions women make in every aspect of life: in the home, on the job, in their communities, as mothers, wives, sisters, daughters, learners, workers, citizens and leaders.

5 It is also a coming together, much the way women come together every day in every country. We come together in fields and in factories. In village markets and supermarkets, in living rooms and board rooms. Whether it is while playing with our children in the park, or washing clothes in a river, or taking a break at the office water cooler, we come together and talk about our
10 aspirations and concerns. And time and again, our talk turns to our children and our families. However different we may be, there is far more that unites us than divides us. We share a common future. And we are here to find common ground so that we may help bring new dignity and respect to women and girls all over the world — and in so doing, bring new strength and stability
15 to families as well.

What we are learning is that if women are healthy and educated, their families will flourish. If women are free from violence, their families will flourish. If women have a chance to work and earn as full and equal partners in society, their families will flourish. And when families flourish, communities and
20 nations will flourish. That is why every woman, every man, every child, every family and every nation on our planet has a stake in the discussion that takes place here. At this very moment, as we sit here, women around the world are giving birth, raising children, cooking meals, washing clothes, cleaning houses, planting crops, working on assembly lines, running
25 companies and running countries.

Women also are dying from diseases that should have been prevented or treated; they are watching their children succumb to malnutrition caused by poverty and economic deprivation; they are being denied the right to go to school by their own fathers and brothers; they are being forced into
30 prostitution, and they are being barred from the bank lending office and

banned from the ballot box. Those of us who have the opportunity to be here have the responsibility to speak for those who could not.

If there is one message that echoes forth from this conference, it is that human rights are women's rights — and women's rights are human rights. Let us not
35 forget that among those rights are the right to speak freely — and the right to be heard.

Families rely on mothers and wives for emotional support and care; families rely on women for labor in the home; and increasingly, families rely on women for income needed to raise healthy children and care for other
40 relatives. As long as discrimination and inequities remain so commonplace around the world — as long as girls and women are valued less, fed less, fed last, overworked, underpaid, not schooled and subjected to violence in and out of their homes — the potential of the human family to create a peaceful, prosperous world will not be realised.

QUESTIONS ON PASSAGE ONE

Marks

(a) "Bolt-on accessory" (line 15); "ghettoise" (line 17).
What idea is common to both of these images? Comment in detail on the effectiveness of one of them.   **(3)**

(b) By referring to the author's word choice, comment on the contrast in style and tone between paragraphs four and five (lines 13–22).   **(4)**

(c) Comment on the tone of "Sorry lassies, say the historians, but you've got to face facts" (line 18).   **(2)**

(d) Explain how the sentence "This is just not the full picture" (line 23) provides a linking function in the argument.   **(2)**

(e) Comment on the sentence structure of lines 29–35 ("What about . . . reprisal").   **(2)**

(f)   Explain how the examples of Anne Leith and Anne McKay contribute to the author's argument.   **(2)**

(g)   The last paragraph contains some observations on the historian's method.

   (i)   What does the author believe that historians should aim to do?   **(1)**

   (ii) What two factors might hold the historians back in achieving this aim?   **(2)**

QUESTIONS ON PASSAGE TWO

(h)   Explain the use of two features of the punctuation in the opening sentence.   **(2)**

(i)   (i)   What is the single main contrast suggested between the various locations listed in lines 6–7?   **(2)**

   (ii) How does the sentence structure reinforce this contrast?   **(2)**

(j)   Look again at the sentence in lines 22–25 ("At this very moment . . . running countries").
Comment on the order in which the various examples are arranged.   **(2)**

(k)   Look at lines 26–31. In your own words, summarise the problems faced by women in some parts of the world.   **(3)**

(l)   Hillary Clinton sums up her message as "human rights are women's rights — and women's rights are human rights." (lines 33–34). With reference to the text, give an example of how the speech argues that an improvement in the status of women would benefit the rest of society.   **(2)**

(m)   In your own words, explain three ways in which families rely on women (lines 37–40).   **(2)**

INTERPRETATION PRACTICE

QUESTIONS ON BOTH PASSAGES

Marks

(n)   What similarities do you notice between the role of women in history, considered in passage one, and the status of women as outlined in passage two?

(3)

(o)   Examine the various methods used by each writer to persuade the reader. Which do you consider more successful? Why?

(4)

Total 40 marks

NOVELS

(In the first passage, by Nigel Nicolson, a regular columnist in the Sunday Telegraph, *the writer discusses his love of reading novels. In the second passage, an extract from her novel,* Northanger Abbey, *Jane Austen explains why she feels novels, and novel-writers, deserve more respect than they normally receive.)*

PASSAGE 1

When you come to think of it, it's amazing that you can gather instant information from rows of small letters printed on a page like this. As you read this, you should be astonished (did you not take it for granted) not by what I have written, but by your ability to understand it by eye alone, without even turning
5 the print into muttered words. The capacity to read is education's most wonderful legacy.

It is a source of constant joy, particularly in book-form. What a convenient thing a book is! What a nice thing, so easily portable, so excellently condensed! The habit of reading is acquired young by almost everyone, first as a duty, then
10 as a pleasure. In my childhood there were good books and bad books. The distinction between them was not moral, but of degree of difficulty. A good book was serious, like *Ivanhoe*, with big slabs of prose between the conversations. A bad book was light and entertaining like *Alice in Wonderland*. We were encouraged to read the good books, while longing to read the bad.

15 Slowly we graduated from E. Nesbit's *The Wouldbegoods* and Richmal Crompton's "William" books (all kids enjoy stories about bad children) to Sherlock Holmes and Anthony Hope, and we were given three tips by my father about our future reading. They were : you can have two books on the go at the same time, but not more; you should finish reading any book if you have not
20 got bored with it by page 36; and you should make, in pencil, personal notes at the back.

This last injunction will seem to many people outrageous. A book should *never* be defaced by the reader's stupid comments. I disagree. I invariably sideline passages that I want to remember, and index them with references like
25 "Funny story, p216" or "good quote, 143", so that when, years later, I pick up

the book again, I can rediscover those passages, and if someone else reads my copy, they will be amused by my reactions.

For most of us, the joy of reading is the pleasure of discovering other people's inventions. You know that you are an addicted reader if you long for the
30 moment when you can decently go to bed and resume the book where you left off the night before, renewing contact with people whom you will never meet in the flesh, but whom you already know better than most of those you will meet in real life.

Hence my delight in Trollope. I am currently reading one of his lesser-known
35 novels, *The American Senator*. I am halfway through (p286), and still do not know whether Arabella will succeed in getting Lord Rufford to marry her. This is the adult equivalent of a "bad" book. It requires from me no mental effort whatever. What do I care? That's what books are for. When I eventually retire, I will read, read, read bad books without any feeling of guilt, and when I drive
40 myself, as I intend, to discover idyllic parts of England before it is too late, I shall listen to spoken-word tapes, provided that they are not of the kind that play spooky music as background to dramatic passages, and soapy music for the sentimental.

And I will read the classics in translation. Proust, in any case, sounds much
45 better in English, and so does Thucydides. There was a terrible woman whom I once knew, who expressed surprise that I was not reading *Anna Karenina* in Russian. "You will lose everything," she said. I didn't.

© Nigel Nicolson

PASSAGE 2

Although our productions have afforded more extensive and unaffected pleasure than those of any other literary corporation in the world, no species of composition has been so much decried. From pride, ignorance or fashion, our foes are almost as many as our readers; and while the abilities of the nine-
5 hundredth abridger of the *History of England*, or of the man who collects and publishes in a volume some dozen lines of Milton, Pope, and Prior, with a paper from *The Spectator*, and a chapter from Sterne, are eulogised by a thousand pens, there seems almost a general wish of undervaluing the labour of the novelist, and of slighting the performances which have only genius, wit, and
10 taste to recommend them.

"I am no novel-reader — I seldom look into novels — Do not imagine that I often read novels — It is really very well for a novel." Such is the common cant.

Continued on next page

"And what are you reading, Miss —— ?"

15 "Oh! it is only a novel!" replies the young lady, while she lays down her book with affected indifference or momentary shame.

It is only *Cecilia* or *Camilla*, or *Belinda*, or, in short, only some work in which the greatest powers of the mind are displayed, in which the most thorough knowledge of human nature, the happiest delineation of its varieties, the liveliest effusions of wit and humour, are conveyed to the world in the best-chosen 20 language. Now, had the same young lady been engaged with a volume of *The Spectator*, instead of such a work, how proudly would she have produced the book, and told its name!

QUESTIONS ON PASSAGE 1

Marks

(a)   In the first paragraph, (lines 1–6), what two things about reading does the author see as amazing?   **(2)**

(b)   In paragraph 2, (lines 7–14), what does the author see as the main advantage of print in book form?   **(2)**

(c)   Look at paragraphs 2 (lines 7–14), and 6 (lines 34–43). Explain in your own words the difference between "good" and "bad" books, according to the author.   **(4)**

(d)   Look at paragraph 3 (lines 15–21). Choose either the **first** or **second** of the author's father's "three tips". Briefly state it in your own words, then give reasons why you do or do not think it good advice.   **(3)**

(e)   Show how the opening sentence of paragraph 4, "This injunction . . . outrageous", acts as a link.   **(2)**

(f)   Look at paragraph 4 (lines 22–27). In your own words, explain how the author justifies his habit of making notes in books.   **(4)**

(g)   "A book should *never* be defaced by the reader's stupid comments." (lines 22 and 23). Describe the author's tone here, explaining your answer.   **(2)**

(h) What clue does the author give in paragraph 5 (lines 28–33) which explains his love of reading? **(2)**

(i) Explain the tone of the words "spooky" and "soapy" (line 42) to describe music on taped books. What is revealed of the author's attitude to such background music? **(2)**

(j) What is the effect of the final short sentence in the last paragraph? **(2)**

QUESTIONS ON PASSAGE 2

(k) Jane Austen shows an awareness of Nigel Nicolson's distinction between "good books" and "bad books". Give an example of each from Passage 2, making clear which is which. **(2)**

(l) What language technique is used in the phrase "the nine-hundredth abridger of the *History of England*"? Comment on its effect. **(2)**

(m) (i) Explain the author's tone in the expression "performances which have only genius, wit, and taste to recommend them" (lines 9–10). **(1)**

(ii) Give another example of this tone from the passage. **(1)**

(n) In the last paragraph, (lines 16–22), the author presents five features of great novels. List these **in your own words**. **(5)**

QUESTION ON BOTH PASSAGES

(o) Using quotations to support your answer, compare and contrast the style of the two passages. You should consider the author's purpose, sentence structure, word choice and tone. (Remember to include similarities as well as differences.) **(4)**

Total 40 marks

GRANDMOTHERS

(The first passage is from Laurie Lee's autobiography, Cider with Rosie, *the story of his boyhood in a Gloucestershire village around the time of the first world war. Passage 2 is adapted from a column by Katherine Whitehorn in* The Observer.*)*

PASSAGE 1

The house next to ours was divided between two old ladies, one's portion lying above the other's. Granny Trill and Granny Wallon were rival ancients and lived on each others' nerves, and their perpetual enmity was like mice in the walls and absorbed much of my early days. With their sickle-bent bodies, pale pink
5 eyes, and wild wisps of hedgerow hair, they looked to me the very images of witches and they were also much alike.

Granny Wallon, who lived on our level, was perhaps the smaller of the two, a tiny white shrew who came nibbling through her garden, who clawed squeaking with gossip at our kitchen window, or sat sucking bread in the sun; always mysterious
10 and self-contained and feather-soft in her movements. Behind this crisp and trotting body were rumours of noble blood. But she never spoke of them herself. She was known to have raised a score of children. And she was known to be very poor. She lived on cabbage, bread and potatoes — but she also made excellent wines.

15 Whatever the small indulgences with which Granny Wallon warmed up her old life, her neighbour, Granny Trill, had none of them. She was as frugal as a sparrow and as simple in her ways as a grub. She could sit in her chair for hours without moving, a veil of blackness over her eyes, a suspension like frost on her brittle limbs, with little to show that she lived at all save the gentle
20 motion of her jaws. One of the first things I noticed about old Granny Trill was that she always seemed to be chewing, sliding her folded gums together in a daylong ruminative cud.

Continued on next page

INTERPRETATION PRACTICE

Granny Trill had an original sense of time which seemed to obey some vestigial
pattern. She breakfasted, for instance, at four in the morning, had dinner at ten,
25 took tea at two-thirty, and was back in her bed at five. Although she had a
clock she kept it simply for the tick, its hands having dropped off years ago.

Snuff was Granny T's horrible vice, and she indulged it with no moderation. A
fine brown dust coated all her clothes and she had nostrils like badgerholes. She
kept her snuff in a small round box, made of tin and worn smooth as a pebble.
30 She was continually tapping and snapping it open, pinching a nailful, gasping
"Ah!", flicking her fingers and wiping her eyes, and leaving on the air a faint
dry cloud like an explosion of fungoid dust.

The snuff-box repelled and excited us boys and we opened its lid with awe.
Reeking substance of the underworld, clay-brown dust of decay, of powdered
35 flesh and crushed old bones, rust-scrapings, and the rubbish of graves. How
sharp and stinging was this fearful spice, eddying up from its box, animating the
air with tingling fumes like a secret breath of witchery.

Granny Trill and Granny Wallon were traditional ancients of a kind we won't
see today. They wore high laced boots and long muslin dresses, beaded chokers
40 and candlewick shawls, crowned by tall poke bonnets tied with trailing ribbons
and smothered with inky sequins. They looked like starlings, flecked with jet,
and they walked in a tinkle of darkness. These severe and similar old bodies
enthralled me when they dressed that way. When I finally became King (I used
to think) I would command a parade of grandmas, and drill them, and march
45 them up and down — rank upon rank of hobbling boots, nodding bonnets, flying
shawls, and furious chewing faces. No more than a monarch's whim, of course,
like eating cocoa or drinking jelly; but far more spectacular any day than those
usual trudging guardsmen.

Extract from Cider With Rosie by Laurie Lee

A good many people don't seem to realise that granny-battering goes on, so it's small wonder they haven't given much thought to what causes it. Of course, there are people whose natural violence spills over against the aged as it might against anyone in the family, child or wife; and you get occasional cases of the

5 Darby and Joan syndrome, in which a lifetime's frustrations and furies finally boil over and Darby finishes off Joan, or vice versa. But what is much more common is women driven to the end of their tether by having an old, demanding and possibly cantankerous parent to look after day and night without any let-up for years.

10 If it is your own old Mum you're looking after, she can be beastly to you with impunity (half the horror stories involve old women who bully their daughters as if they were children). If, however, it's someone else's Mum and you're doing it as a job, even an unpaid one, then she becomes someone you cope with for four hours or eight, knowing you can go home to a bit of sanity and privacy.

15 A recent TV series contrasted the cheery acceptance of old people's foibles by professionals and home helps with the awful burden of guilt and emotional blackmail that goes on in the family.

At a conference last week I was listening to an official of a Health Authority explaining that people would have to work for free to look after old people,

20 since there was no chance that the State would ever now come up with enough money. I became fairly furious as heads nodded approvingly in a room in which only about a dozen people there were ever likely to get stuck with this chore, the rest being men.

You'd have thought by now that the farce of community care was an exploded myth,

25 that no one could seriously be recommending more of it as an answer to anything; but I suppose there are still people who think it means something other than finding the nearest female and sticking her with it. However, he went on to establish that he didn't mean just this, but some sort of an extension of voluntary work. And here perhaps there just might be the germ of a solution.

30 What about linking a stint at the coal-face of community care to the first five or 10 years of receiving an old age pension? Not full-time. Not in rotten

INTERPRETATION PRACTICE

conditions. Not replacing other existing workers. But giving, say, 10 hours a week for the first five or 10 years after retirement to whatever community provision there was for the old and senile, the handicapped, or any of the other 35 categories of people now driving their mothers and daughters round the bend.

To such newly-retired people, looking after those who needed it would be a job, like any other job; not a nightmare of never-ending obligation.

QUESTIONS ON PASSAGE 1

Marks

(a) Animal images are frequently used to describe the "grannies" in paragraphs 1, 2 and 3. Pick out two examples, each from a different paragraph. Explain what impression each of the images conveys to you, making clear whether you find them pleasant or unpleasant.

(4)

(b) Explain how the first sentence of paragraph 3 (lines 15–16) forms a link between paragraphs 2 and 3.

(2)

(c) Comment on the structure of the sentence "She was continually . . . fungoid dust". (lines 30–32). Say what effect you think the author was trying to achieve.

(2)

(d) Look at paragraph 6 (lines 33–37). "The snuff-box repelled . . . witchery". Explain how the choice of vocabulary and imagery accurately convey the boys' feelings of both repulsion and excitement.

(4)

(e) How does the sentence in brackets in lines 43–44 affect your response to the passage as a whole, and its view of "grannies"?

(2)

QUESTIONS ON PASSAGE 2

Marks

(f)   (i)   "Granny-battering" (line 1). From where do you think the author has derived this word? **(1)**

       (ii)   What effect do you think this expression has on the reader? **(2)**

(g)   Comment on the structure of the last sentence of paragraph 1 (lines 6–9): "But what is much more common . . . years". Explain how the structure chosen is appropriate to the ideas. **(2)**

(h)   Look at the opening sentence of paragraph 2: "If it is your own old Mum . . . children)." There is a contrast in style between the phrases "your own old Mum" and "with impunity". Explain the contrast, and say what effect the author achieves by using the two styles throughout the passage. **(3)**

(i)   In paragraph 2, (lines 10–17), caring for the elderly is seen as less stressful for professional carers than for relatives. What reasons are suggested for this? **(4)**

(j)   Look at paragraph 3 (lines 18–23). Explain the difference in the perceived roles of men and women in caring for the elderly. **(2)**

(k)   Sum up in your own words, in formal continuous prose, the main features of the author's scheme for providing care for the elderly. **(4)**

QUESTIONS ON BOTH PASSAGES

(l)   The passages offer two different attitudes towards the elderly. Referring to the word choice of both passages, sum up the two attitudes and say which is closer to your own view, giving brief reasons. **(4)**

(m)   Referring closely to the text of both passages, sum up what you see as the problems that might arise when caring for the elderly within the family. **(4)**

Total 40 marks

INTERPRETATION PRACTICE

INTERPRETATION PRACTICE (4)

AMERICA AND THE AMERICANS

PASSAGE 1

In this extract from his autobiography, Memory Hold-the-Door, *John Buchan (1875–1940) discusses his view of the characteristics of American people.*

Let me try to set down certain qualities which seem to me to flourish more lustily in the United States than elsewhere. Again, let me repeat, I speak of America only as I know it; an observer with different experience might not agree with my conclusions.

5 First, I would select what, for want of a better word, I should call homeliness. It is significant that the ordinary dwelling, though it be only a shack in the woods, is called not a house, but a home. This means that the family, the ultimate social unit, is given its proper status as the foundation of society. It is often said that Americans are a nomad race, and it is true that they are very

10 ready to shift their camp; but the camp, however bare, is always a home. The cohesion of the family is close, even when its members are scattered. This is due partly to the tradition of the first settlers, a handful in an unknown land; partly to the history of the frontier, where a hearth-fire burnt brighter when all around was cold and darkness. The later immigrants from Europe, feeling

15 at last secure, were able for the first time to establish a family base, and they cherished it zealously. This ardent domesticity has had its bad effects on American literature, inducing a sentimentality which makes a too crude frontal attack on the emotions, and which has produced as a reaction a not less sentimental "toughness". But as a social cement it is beyond price.

20 Second, I would choose the sincere and widespread friendliness of the people. Americans are interested in the human race, and in each other. Deriving doubtless from the old frontier days, there is a general helpfulness, which I have not found in the same degree elsewhere. A homesteader in Dakota will accompany a traveller for miles to set him on the right road. The neighbours

25 will rally round one of their number in distress with the loyalty of a Highland clan. This friendliness is not a self-conscious duty so much as an instinct. A squatter in a cabin will share his scanty provisions and never dream that he is doing anything unusual.

American hospitality, long as I have enjoyed it, still leaves me breathless.
30 The lavishness with which a busy man will give up precious time to entertain a stranger to whom he is in no way bound remains for me one of the wonders of the world.

No doubt this friendliness, since it is an established custom, has its false side. The endless brotherhoods into which people brigade themselves encourage a
35 geniality which is more a mannerism than an index of character, a tiresome, noisy, back-slapping heartiness. But that is the exception, not the rule.

Lastly — and this may seem a paradox — I maintain that Americans are fundamentally modest. As a nation they are said to be sensitive to criticism; that surely is modesty, for the truly arrogant care nothing for the opinions of
40 other people. Above all they can laugh at themselves, which is not possible for the immodest. They are their own shrewdest and most ribald critics. It is charged against them that they are inclined to boast unduly about those achievements and about the greatness of their country, but a smug glorying in them is found only in the American of the caricaturist.

In this article from The Guardian, *John Cunningham considers the dangers of living in New York today.*

In a third floor window facing the main bus station in Manhattan, a neon sign says "Jesus Cares". As the evening rush shoals into the terminal on Eighth Avenue, He's probably the only one who does. The terminal is the hang-out of drug-pushers, hustlers, panhandlers and all kinds of crazies. Mid-town
5 professionals have developed a street-smart defence: avoid all eye contact and move smartly between destinations in case the desperate dispossessed in their hi-top trainers and sweat pants turn nasty. Once-blasé New York now fears the violence is turning it into a city besieged by its own lawless inhabitants.

As the polluted air eats into the decaying buildings, the poisoned atmosphere
10 of social relations is crumbling the confidence of the city itself. The defiant assertions of new buildings like Trump Tower and the World Trade Centre deny that anything is amiss, but everyone knows that Donald Trump still stands at all only because his collapse would cause an earthquake under the American banking giants; just as the yuppies, staking out Central Park on crisp, autumn
15 Sundays as a huge health club, have fixed in their minds the horrendous attack on a woman jogger, a Wall Street executive raped and left for dead in a "wilding" attack by a gang of teenagers. The mask has dropped from the face of capitalism's hi-tech, can-do city to reveal how little separates Manhattan from a third-world shanty capital.

20 Criminal violence, deliberate and random, has become so hi-risk that many residents consider the Big Apple uninhabitable. The fall term has dictated a new fashion in uniforms for school children — bullet-proof clothes — and added a new lesson to the timetable — urban survival. The toll of murders, robberies and rapes is disabling a city that likes to stride tall.

25 Many newcomers no longer have aspirations of struggle and self-improvement — the common virtue which bound the huddled polyglot masses arriving in the period of mass migration from 1880 to 1910. Where once immigrants

brought their skills, now they bring their guile, in the worst sense. As if to
recall a better-motivated American, Ellis Island, the main entry point for
30 immigrants since the last century, was opened as a monument in September.
From the first day it opened, descendants of immigrants have been queueing to
visit the restored buildings. As a symbol to uplift New York, it is probably
more effective than Mayor Dinkins preaching against civic disorder in St.
John's Cathedral, or civic leaders attending the funerals of murder victims.
35 Confused New York needs to recall a time when crime was of manageable
proportions. If only to convince itself that the Big Apple has not gone rotten.

QUESTIONS ON PASSAGE 1

Marks

(a)   What does the author state the main purpose of the passage to be?   **(1)**

(b)   Basing your answer on lines 7 and 8, explain the author's reasons for
mentioning the fact that "the ordinary dwelling is called not a house but a
home."   **(2)**

(c)   What is meant by a "nomad race" (line 9)? Explain how the context of the
phrase helps you to arrive at the meaning.   **(3)**

(d)   Look at lines 16–19. Explain ONE of the effects the love of "domesticity" had
on American literature.   **(2)**

(e)   (i)   Explain the distinction between "duty" and "instinct" (line 26).   **(2)**

   (ii)   Which of the examples given makes this distinction particularly clear?   **(2)**

(f)   "No doubt this friendliness, since it is an established custom, has its false side"
(line 33).

Explain how this sentence provides a linking function in the development of the
argument of the passage.   **(2)**

(g)   What evidence is there in the last paragraph for the author's belief that the
Americans are "fundamentally modest"?   **(3)**

(h) The author tends to explain his view of contemporary Americans in terms of their ancestors. Using your owns words, illustrate this comment by reference to one example from the extract.

(3)

QUESTIONS ON PASSAGE TWO

(i) Comment on the effectiveness of the metaphor "the mask has dropped from the face" (lines 17–18) and show how this relates to the ideas contained in the second paragraph.

(3)

(j) Look at the final paragraph of the extract.

(i) Explain in your own words what it was that immigrants to America shared in the first period of mass migration.

(2)

(ii) Explain the change which the writer claims has occurred amongst present-day immigrants.

(2)

(iii) Quote an expression which reveals the writer's attitude to these more recent immigrants.

(1)

(k) Explain why Ellis Island would be effective as "a symbol to uplift New York" (line 32).

(2)

(l) Comment on either the structure or the imagery of the final sentence and discuss its effectiveness as an ending.

(3)

QUESTIONS ON BOTH PASSAGES

(m) Each writer presents a view of American society. Comment on any two differences or on any two similarities in the ways the writers present the subject, using quotations to illustrate your comments.

(4)

(n) Which of the two writers seems to you to present a more convincing description of the Americans? Justify your answer by close reference to the text of both passages.

(3)

Total 40 marks

APPENDICES

Appendix I: Grammar and Syntax

As was explained earlier, questions on sentence structure require you to demonstrate your understanding of how language is put together — how paragraphs and sentences are assembled. The technical terms for this are **grammar** and **syntax**. "Syntax" is the arrangement of words and phrases in a sentence, and "grammar" is the body of rules according to which such arrangements are made.

Writers aim to achieve certain effects through syntax, and you will be expected to recognise, identify and explain these techniques. Obviously, the more you know about grammar and syntax, the better able you will be to appreciate their particular application within writers' work. The following section will give you a brief summing up of some of the basic principles of grammar and it will explain some of the terminology which is used.

Sentences, Clauses and Phrases

A **sentence** is a group of words which contains a verb, and makes complete sense. A sentence may be a **statement**, a **question**, an **exclamation** or a **command**: "John is sitting down." "Is John sitting down?" "John is sitting down!" "Sit down, John."

Although **sentence analysis** is often regarded as old-fashioned and has been widely discarded from the English syllabus, a basic knowledge *is* useful, and can enable you to discuss an author's techniques with more authority. You may be able to note if a part of a sentence seems to be missing, or if a sentence has an unusual formation.

Firstly, a sentence can be split into various elements. The **subject** is the topic which is being discussed. The **predicate** is what is said about the "subject". It contains the verb of the sentence.

Here are three examples of sentences, which all happen to have the same subject.

Subject	Predicate
The dog	killed the rat. gave his master the stick. ran across the road.

"Predicate" is not in itself a particularly useful term, but an analysis of different patterns of predicate can be helpful.

Firstly, the predicate always contains the **verb** of the sentence: "killed", "gave" and "ran" in the previous examples.

The first predicate contains the verb "killed" plus a **direct object** "the rat". This answers the question "*What* did the dog kill?"

The second predicate also contains a verb "gave" and a direct object "the stick" which answers the question "What did the dog give?" It also contains an **indirect object** "his master". This answers the question "To whom?".

Verbs which make sense when followed with a direct object, as in these two examples, are called "**transitive**" verbs.

Some verbs do not require a direct object to make sense. These are called **intransitive** verbs. Predicate number three contains such a verb. The question "What?" does not make sense after "the dog ran . . .". This predicate is completed with an adverbial phrase "across the road". Such a phrase will answer the question "Where", "When" or "How". Adverbial phrases can also be used in sentences with transitive verbs.

FOR PRACTICE

Draw a table with five columns, like the one below, and then analyse the following sentences. Remember that you will not have something in each column every time.

Subject	Verb	Direct Object	Indirect Object	Adverbial Phrase

(a) I told the children a story.
(b) The light shone into the room.
(c) The aircraft crashed just after take-off.
(d) She found the missing money in the tea-caddy.

Word Order

As discussed on page 23, the normal word order in English is for the subject to come first, then the predicate:

> A stranger stood in the doorway.

However, occasionally the subject is delayed and placed after part of the predicate or even after the whole of the predicate, a technique known as **inversion**:

> In the doorway stood a stranger.

The use of inversion subtly alters the emphasis. In the above example, for instance, the use of inversion adds more suspense as the phrase "a stranger" is delayed slightly, which throws the spotlight onto it.

FOR PRACTICE

Consider what effect is obtained in the following examples of inversion. (The conventional word order is given first for purposes of comparison.) Remember that there will only be a *slight* difference, perhaps of tone or emphasis.

1. (a) His fist smacked down onto the table.
    (b) Down smacked his fist onto the table.

2. (a) The car door opened and the Queen stepped out.
    (b) The car door opened and out stepped the Queen.

3   (a) A beautiful princess lived in a dark and gloomy castle in the middle of a dense forest.
    (b) In the middle of a dense forest, in a dark and gloomy castle, lived a beautiful princess.

4. (a) I have never done that.
    (b) That, I have never done.

5. (a) For Henry Jekyll stood there before my eyes, pale and shaken, and half fainting and groping before him with his hands like a man restored from death!
    (b) For there before my eyes — pale and shaken, and half fainting, and groping before him with his hands like a man restored from death — there stood Henry Jekyll!

Active or passive?

Another variation which alters the emphasis in a sentence is the use of the so-called **passive voice**. Usually, the subject performs the action of the verb. But this need not be so.

For example, the sentence
> The lion killed the zebra

could be rearranged to:
> The zebra was killed by the lion.

In this sentence "the zebra" is grammatically the subject, although the action was done to it. Using the passive voice suggests that the zebra, however, is the main focus of interest.

Notice that the passive often has an **impersonal** tone: this is a construction often used in reports and other situations where formal language is desirable, e.g.,

> *It was agreed* that the meeting should be adjourned.

This is preferred to the more personal, active form : "We agreed that . . ." or "People agreed that . . ." These would sound less formal and official.

Clauses; Complex and simple sentences.

A sentence is composed of one or more "clauses". A **clause** is a unit of language containing a subject and a predicate. A **simple** sentence contains one clause only:

> The lion killed the zebra.

A **complex** sentence contains more than one clause, but at least one of these must make sense by itself:

> Because it needed food for its cubs, the lion killed the zebra.

In this example, the clause "the lion killed the zebra" could make sense by itself. Such a clause is known as the **principal** or **main** clause. Clauses which cannot stand alone, as in this example, "because it needed food for its cubs", are called "subordinate" clauses.

(A distinction is sometimes made between complex sentences and compound, the latter containing more than one principal clause. In practice this distinction is unlikely to be useful.)

The sentence structure chosen will reflect the subject matter. For example, a series of short, simple sentences may build up tension. A single simple sentence may make a very dramatic contrast after a series of longer ones. A climax may be built up or a surprise created by a series of subordinate clauses followed by a main clause. Sometimes a number of simple sentences (each a principal clause) are strung together with "ands". This is known as a "loose" sentence structure. It is used in informal writing or writing that is being made deliberately simple — to suggest boredom, for example.

Subordinate clauses can function as nouns, adjectives or adverbs. Although you will not be asked to identify types of clauses, it can be useful to be able to do so.

(a)   A noun clause answers the question "What?" in response to a main clause. It is usually introduced by "that" or "what", e.g.:

> He told me *that he would be unable to come.*
> I asked him *what he was doing.*

(b)   An adjective clause describes something or someone and is usually introduced by "who", "whom", "which" or (less commonly) "that", e.g.:

> The man *who lives next door* has just won the lottery.
> I lost the book *which I had borrowed from the library.*

(c)   Adverbial clauses are of many types and perform various functions. The following four types are among the most common and the most useful to be able to recognise.

   (i)   Time (answers the question "When?"): introduced by "when", "before", "after", e.g.:
   > *When the cat's away,* the mice will play.

   (ii)   Condition (answers the question "On what condition?) introduced by "if" or "unless", e.g.:
   > *If I see him* I will tell him.

   (iii)   Reason (answers the question "Why?") introduced by "because", "as", "since", e.g.:
   > He went home from work *because he felt ill.*

   (iv)   Concession (answers the question "In spite of what?") introduced by "although", e.g.:
   > *Although he was small,* he was strong.

Phrases

A phrase is a group of words, not including a verb, which forms a unit. For example:

> a fat, black cat
> with long, fair hair
> slowly but surely
> in the corner of the room
> next Tuesday

Phrases can be used as nouns, adjectives and adverbs. (In the list above, the first example is a noun phrase, the second is an adjectival phrase and the other three are adverbial phrases: of manner, place and time respectively.)

You might notice that a sentence contains a number of one type of phrase, for example. You could note this and suggest the effect the writer is aiming at.

Parts of Speech

Parts of speech is the term given to words according to their function in a piece of writing. The terminology used for this varies, but the traditional method is perhaps the simplest. This includes **nouns** (common, proper, collective, abstract), **verbs, adjectives, adverbs, pronouns, prepositions, conjunctions and articles.)**

Verbs, perhaps, offer the widest scope for comment. Using many action verbs may create a tense, dynamic effect: e.g.:

> "He *raced* down the hall, *wrenched* open the door, *leapt* down the porch steps and *flung* himself into his car."

You should be able to recognise **present participles** (which end in -ing). Repeated use of these creates a sense of prolonged or continuing action. Verb **tenses** (past, present and future) may be worthy of comment. The tense used in most narrative is past, but occasionally a "historic present" is used which adds immediacy or drama to the writing. (See Example 5, below.) We have noted above how a verb may be **active** or **passive**, and it may also be in the form of a **command**, e.g.: "*Buy* British!".

Adjectives have three forms: **positive**, **comparative** and **superlative** (as in big — bigger — biggest). Frequent use of comparatives and superlatives is typical of writing which aims to persuade, such as travel brochures or advertisements.

Conjunctions are important. We have already seen (in the section on Understanding the Meaning) how conjunctions indicate the linkage of ideas in an argument. The use of "and" is often particularly significant. It may be omitted where it would normally be expected, which usually has a terse, dramatic effect:

"I came, I saw, I conquered",

or it may be repeated more frequently than usual. In the following example, the "ands" emphasise the tediousness of a dinner party:

"The Professor was charming and attentive and told Dolly that he liked her hat, and Mrs Clifford seemed really interested in life at the Coombe Hotel and wanted to hear all about the people who lived there."

Extract from *The Shell Seekers* by Rosamunde Pilcher

It is impossible to cover all the variations which are to be found in the way parts of speech are used, but you should be on the alert for parts of speech used in an unusual way and be prepared to comment. Some writers will have typical mannerisms. One writer habitually uses lists of adjectives without including "and", frequently in groups of three to create a small climax:

"He left the room depressed, dejected, despairing."

FOR PRACTICE

Comment on the authors' use of sentence structure in the following pieces of writing and consider their purpose in the techniques they have chosen. You could also comment on any other striking features of style such as word choice or imagery.

1. (*In the following extract, the character is extremely dissatisfied and bored with life.*)
    The flat crouched around him, watching like a depressed relation, waiting for him to take some action. He drew the curtains and switched on the lamp and things looked marginally better. He took *The Times* from his coat pocket and tossed it on the table. Pulled off his coat and flung it across a chair. He went into the kitchen and poured a strong whisky and filled the glass with ice from the fridge. He went back to the sitting room and sat down on the sofa and opened the paper.

    Extract from *The Shell Seekers* by Rosamunde Pilcher

2. At evening, sitting on this terrace,
    When the sun from the west, beyond Pisa, beyond the mountains of Carrara
    Departs, and the world is taken by surprise . . .

    Look up, and you see things flying
    Between the day and the night.

    Extract from *Bat* by D.H. Lawrence

3. *In the following extract two sisters have gone down to a creek for a picnic. When they return home they find that one of the sisters has lost a valuable brooch borrowed from her mother without permission, and so they must carefully retrace their exact steps.*

    Back we went, searching the bush on which the meadow lark had sung, following our faint trail through the waving grass, refinding the places where the violets. were thickest. Down we went on our hands and knees, pushing aside the slim, cool grass with edges that cut the fingers.

    Extract from *Tall Grass* by Maureen Daly

4. The court was told that Miss Martin had not been at home on the Saturday evening. It was alleged that the accused had entered her house and waited there for her to return. He was said to have threatened her with a knife when she opened the door and forced her to reveal where the safe was. Money and jewellery to the value of five thousand pounds were handed over by Miss Martin who was then tied to a chair. The alarm was raised at midnight, when the friend with whom she had spent the evening telephoned and received no reply.

5. In a public lavatory, with the door locked, Felicia feels her way through the belongings in the heavier of her carrier bags, to the jersey in which she has secreted the greater part of her money. She has two pounds and seventy-three pence left in the purse in her handbag.

    But the sleeves of the jersey are empty and, thinking she has made a mistake, she searches the other bag. Since it yields nothing either, she returns to the first one. In a panic she takes everything out of both, littering the floor of the cubicle, unfolding the navy-blue jersey and shaking out all the other clothes. The money is not there.

    Extract from *Felicia's Journey* by William Trevor

6. Capri is essentially a fairy tale, a dream lost in the extraordinary azure of an incredible sea, in the boundless panoramas which embrace other precious tesserae of that wonderful mosaic which is the Neapolitan and Salerno coast, between Capo Miseno and Amalfi. Everything which can be perceived by the senses finds its greatest elevation on this island; from the light, sublime complement and refined facets of colour which allow one to read, as in an open book, the endless wonders of the place; from the perfume of the flowers which constitutes another jewel of the island and the vegetation which is a mixture of Mediterranean aspects and more precisely tropical ones: from the strong salt-laden breezes of a sea which is the very life of the island; from the disturbing voice of silence, broken only by the piercing cry of the seagulls and the breaking of the waves on the steep and precipitous rocks; from the possibility of touching with one's own hands the ancient traces of an illustrious and fascinating history, together with numerous remains of a past which represents the most authentic cultural matrix of the place.

    Extract from *Capri Gold Guide*

Appendix II: Sources

The following are the sources of the extracts on pages 59 – 65.

1.   *A Brief History of Time* © Stephen Hawking 1988

   Non-fiction : Physics presented for the layman supposedly in simple and non-technical language.

2.   *The Tailor of Gloucester* by Beatrix Potter © Frederick Warne & Co.

   A book for very young children in which animals behave like humans; written in 1901.

3.   *The Crow Road* © Iain Banks 1992

   A contemporary thriller with strong elements of black comedy.

4.   *Wild Swans* by Jung Chang © Globalflair Ltd. 1991

   An autobiography by a contemporary Chinese writer.

5.   *Odysseus* © Tony Robinson and Richard Curtis 1986

   A humorous version of Homer's Odyssey (an epic in Ancient Greek) aimed at older children.

6.   *Class* © Jilly Cooper 1980

   Non-fiction : a light-hearted and entertaining examination of the social class system in Britain.

7.   *The Mysteries of Udolpho* by Mrs. Ann Radcliffe

   A Gothic romance written in 1794.

8.   *The Kingdom by the Sea* © Paul Theroux 1984

      Non-fiction : an American's view of Britain as seen from a tour around its coasts.

9.   *The Rosewell Incident* © Irvine Welsh

      A short story with an element of science fiction.

10.   *The Crystal Bucket* © Clive James 1982

      A selection of television criticism from the writer's regular column in *The Observer.*

11.   *All Quiet on the Western Front* © Erich Maria Remarque

      Set during the first world war, this is an anti-war novel by a German writer based on personal experience.

12.   *Glasgow for Free* © Debra Shipley and Mary Peplow 1988

      Non-fiction : an informal guide to those of Glasgow's attractions which are available to the visitor free of charge.

13.   *Kenilworth* by Sir Walter Scott

      A historical novel, written in 1821, but set in 1560. Scott writes in deliberately archaic language, in attempting to capture the idiom of Elizabethan times.

Acknowledgements

We are extremely grateful to the following for permission to use copyright material in this book.

Extract from *The Story of Art* by E.H. Grombrich.
Reproduced from *The Story of Art* by Professor E.H. Gombrich © 1995 Phaidon Press Limited.

Extract from *Odysseus* by Robinson Curtis.
Reproduced by permission of BBC Worldwide.

Extract from *Nothing like a good book — or bad one* by Nigel Nicolson.
Reproduced by permission of the author Nigel Nicholson.

Extract from *Notes from a Small Island* © Bill Bryson 1995.
Published by Black Swan, a division of Transworld Publishers Ltd. All rights reserved.

Extract from *Cold Comfort Farm* by Stella Gibbons.
Reproduced by permission of the publisher, Penguin UK Ltd.

Extract from *Kingdom by the Sea* by Paul Theroux.
Reproduced by permission of the publisher, Penguin Books Ltd.

Extract from *Empire of the Sun* by J.G. Ballard published by Harper Collins, Publishers.

Extract from *Mary Queen of Scots* by Antonia Fraser.
Reproduced by permission of the publisher, Weidenfeld and Nicolson.

Extract from *Homage to Catalonia* by George Orwell.
© Mark Hamilton as the Literary Executor of the Estate of the Late Sonia Brownell Orwell.
Reproduced by permission of Martin Secker & Warburg Ltd and A.M. Heath & Co. Ltd.

Extract from *Cider with Rosie* by Laurie Lee.
Reproduced by permission of the publisher Hogarth Press.

Extract from *History — We need the full picture* by Maggie Craig published in *The Herald*.
Reproduced by permission of the publisher, Scottish Media Group.

Extract from *Idle thoughts* by Laurie Maguire.
Reproduced by courtesy of *The Scotsman*.

Extract from *The Spoils of Childhood* © Libby Purves 1997.
First Published in *The Times*. Reprinted by permission of the author, Libby Purves, and Lisa Eveleigh.

Extract from *The Crystal Bucket* by Clive James.
Reproduced by permission of the publisher Jonathan Cape Ltd.

Extract from *The Mysteries of Udolpho* by Mrs. Ann Radcliffe.
Reproduced by permission of the publisher Oxford University Press.

Extract from *The Tailor of Gloucester* by Beatrix Potter © Frederick Warne & Co., 1903.
Reproduced by permission of the publisher Frederick Warne & Co.

Extract from *Vet in a Spin* by James Herriot.
Reproduced by permission of the publisher Michael Joseph.

The publishers have wherever possible acknowledged the source of copyright material. They regret any inadvertent omission and will be pleased to make the necessary acknowledgement in future printings.